W9-ANB-144

Feathered
Dinosaurs

Titles in THE DINOSAUR LIBRARY Series

THE DINOSAUR LIBRARY

Feathered Dinosaurs

The Origin of Birds

Thom Holmes and Laurie Holmes

Illustrated by Michael William Skrepnick

Series Advisor:
Dr. Peter Dodson
Professor of Veterinary Anatomy and Paleontology,
University of Pennsylvania
and
co-editor of *The Dinosauria*,
the leading reference used by dinosaur scientists

Enslow Publishers, Inc.

40 Industrial Road	PO Box 38
Box 398	Aldershot
Berkeley Heights, NJ 07922	Hants GU12 6BP
USA	UK

http://www.enslow.com

Library of Congress Cataloging-in-Publication Data

Holmes, Thom.
    Feathered dinosaurs : the origin of birds / Thom Holmes and Laurie Holmes ;
illustrated by Michael William Skrepnick.
        p. cm. — (The dinosaur library)
        Includes bibliographical references and index.
        Summary: Explores the connection between birds and dinosaurs, details the time
and areas where these dinosaurs roamed, as well as what they ate and how they
behaved, and discusses major related fossil discoveries.
        ISBN 0-7660-1454-1
        1. Dinosaurs—Juvenile literature. 2. Birds, Fossil—Juvenile literature.
3. Birds—Origin—Juvenile literature. [1. Dinosaurs. 2. Birds, Fossil. 3. Birds.]
    I. Holmes, Laurie. II. Skrepnick, Michael William, ill. III. Title.
QE861.5 .H64   2002
567.9—dc21
                                                                            2001005940

Printed in the United States of America

10 9 8 7 6 5 4 3 2 1

Illustration Credits: Michael William Skrepnick

Photo Credits: © 2001 American Museum of Natural History, pp. 56, 64; © Corel
Corporation, pp. 8–9, 15, 48; Wayne Grady, p. 6 (Thom Holmes); Shaina Holmes,
p. 6 (Laurie Holmes); Thom Holmes, pp. 29, 66, 84, 88; Nanjing Institute of
Geology and Paleontology, p. 58; Michael Tropea, p. 7.

Cover Illustration: Michael William Skrepnick. Illustration depicts *Sinosauropteryx*.

CONTENTS

About the Authors

Thom Holmes is a natural history writer specializing in dinosaur science. He has dug for dinosaurs with leading paleontologists in the United States and South America. He has collaborated with Dr. Peter Dodson on several dinosaur-related projects during the past fifteen years.

Laurie Holmes is a science writer and editor, as well as a reading specialist. It has been her privilege to associate with many of the world's leading dinosaur scientists and artists through her work with her husband, Thom. Originally a teacher, she maintains that she is still teaching by writing and editing books for young adults.

On a dig in Patagonia, Thom Holmes holds part of the skull bone of what is currently known as the largest meat-eating dinosaur ever.

Thom Holmes   Laurie Holmes

Authors' Note

Dinosaurs hold a special fascination for people all over the world. In writing *The Dinosaur Library*, we enjoyed sharing the knowledge that allows scientists to understand what dinosaurs were really like. You will learn about the differences that make groups of dinosaurs unique, as well as the many similarities that dinosaurs shared.

The Dinosaur Library covers all the suborders of dinosaurs, from the meat-eating theropods, such as *Tyrannosaurus rex*, to the gigantic plant eaters. We hope you enjoy learning about these fascinating creatures that ruled the earth for 160 million years.

About the Illustrator

Michael William Skrepnick is an established paleo artist with a lifelong interest in dinosaurs. He has worked on newly described dinosaurs with a number of the world's leading paleontologists. His original artworks are found in a number of art collections and reproduced as museum murals, and in popular books, magazines, scientific journals, and television documentaries.

Michael lives and works in Alberta, Canada, close to some of the richest Upper Cretaceous dinosaur fossil localities in the world.

Paleo art is a field devoted to the reconstruction and life restoration of long extinct animals and their environments. Since we cannot observe dinosaurs (other than living birds) in nature, we may never truly know their habits, lifestyles, or the color of their skin. In addition, the fossil record provides only a fraction of the remains of a wide diversity of life on earth.

Many fairly complete skeletons of dinosaurs have been unearthed in recent history. Others are represented by as little as a fragment of a single fractured bone, an isolated tooth, or a footprint impressed in once-wet mud. It is still possible to create a reliable portrait of unique, previously unknown creatures, but the accuracy of the art depends on the following:

- The quality and amount of actual skeletal material of the specimen preserved
- Discussion and collaboration with a paleontologist familiar with the fossil material and locality from which it was excavated
- Observation and comparisons to the closest related living forms
- The technical abilities, skill, and disciplined vision of the artist

The resulting artwork can draw the viewer back in time into exotic worlds of the ancient.

SURVIVAL OF THE SMALLEST

As he had been doing every morning, the young Jeholodens *followed his mother out of the damp burrow in which they had slept. The sun was still low on the horizon and its light was filtered by the canopy of cypress and fern trees that hung over the small animals' heads. The youngster sniffed the stalk of a short plant growing in the muddy soil. The main stem of the plant had rows of leafy pods running up the sides. The pods were fat with seeds, one of the foods that* Jeholodens *enjoyed eating. The young one was only a few inches long, and try as he may, his sprawling back legs did not let him raise up high enough to snatch one of the pods. His rat-sized mother noticed the smell of seeds as well and came over to help. She rose up on her hind legs and leaned on the short plant with her front legs until the stalk bent to the ground and snapped. The two of them enjoyed a good meal of seeds.*

Jeholodens *was a mammal living in the shadow of many larger creatures, including dinosaurs. It led a secretive life, staying under cover most of the time, avoiding the sharp eyes of predators that stalked the wooded area for food. The forest was rich with feathered dinosaurs, lizards, birds, and reptiles that would make a quick meal of Jeholodens if they had a chance. But it was the dinosaurs that made Jeholodens the most nervous.*

The two little mammals sat in the shadows eating the seeds. The seeds made a quiet cracking sound as they were broken by the animals' teeth. The nibbling caught the attention of another curious, hungry creature. This one had learned that a meal was nearby when it heard the cracking sound of seeds. It was not after seeds, though. It was after the Jeholodens themselves.

As the predator walked softly in the direction of the Jeholodens, it stepped carefully on the carpet of the forest to avoid making unnecessary noise. The forest was alive with sounds. Birds and insects called from many distances. The sound of water lapping on the shoreline was distant but constant. A soft breeze occasionally swept through the trees with a burst of energy, rustling the branches and leaves.

The predator continued to make its careful approach. It was nearing the spot from which the sound of cracking seeds was coming. The spot was underneath a small clump of ferns that fanned out, hiding the ground.

The mother Jeholodens had noticed the sound of the predator approaching. The footsteps had a kind of rhythm that filled an empty spot in the sounds of her world. Jeholodens had learned that the sound meant danger. When the predator found itself hovering directly over the location of the seed feast, it stopped in its tracks and readied to pounce.

The mother Jeholodens *noticed that the footsteps had stopped. It was time to make their escape. She dropped her seeds and bolted directly into their burrow, with the little one close behind. Only a split second later, the predator reached out with its long feathery arms and brushed aside the ferns that had been shielding the two* Jeholodens. *As it did so, it also lunged forward with its toothy beak, hoping to snatch one of the furry little creatures that it sometimes found in this way. But on this occasion, none was there to be eaten.*

The young Jeholodens *glimpsed back curiously from the mouth of its burrow. It saw the swift flash of two colorfully feathered arms sweep away the ferns and the small fuzzy head of the dinosaur as it snapped desperately at nothing but a few partially eaten seedpods. The eyes of the dinosaur were round and huge. Its body was covered with the same downy fuzz as its head, and its tail was adorned with large colorful feathers like its arms. It stood for a little while, scratching at the ground with its large, three-clawed feet, hoping to find something of interest to eat.*

Jeholodens *had learned to avoid the creatures with feathers. This was difficult because the feathered creatures were swift and cunning. Some of them could silently swoop down in an instant from the air, reaching out with their sharp claws to snatch up unsuspecting creatures. Others, like the* Caudipteryx *that had just threatened them, walked the ground, sniffing and poking around for anything that moved. The best defense for* Jeholodens *was to hide underneath the ceiling of trees and other plants that sheltered the forest ground.*

In a little while the Caudipteryx *could be seen crashing*

through a barrier of ferns in pursuit of a small lizard that was sunning itself on a rock near the lake. The Caudipteryx stood between the edge of the forest and the lizard, cutting off the little reptile's escape route to the woods. The lizard ran along the narrow beach with the feathered dinosaur in pursuit. When the lizard tried to shake its pursuer by making a quick turn, Caudipteryx turned quickly, gliding through the air momentarily,

using its feathered arms to steer itself. As quick as the lizard was, it could not run very fast for long. Without being able to get to the woods, it eventually slowed from exhaustion. When this happened, Caudipteryx was quick to reach out with its long arms and sweep up its prey with its claws. The lizard made for a quick meal.

As it strutted its way back up the sandy beach, the

Caudipteryx *passed the remains of another of its kind that had recently died there. Its body was drying in the sun, its head pulled back in a death pose as the tissue in its neck dried up. Feathers littered the site. The carcass was already half buried by sand from the overnight tide. In another day or so, it would no longer be visible.*

Authors' Note—The preceding story is fiction but is based on scientific evidence and ideas suggested by paleontologists. It depicts what life may have been like in the Liaoning region of northeastern China about 125 million years ago. You will find explanations to support these ideas in the chapters that follow.

CHAPTER 1

DINOSAURS AND BIRDS

Dinosaurs appeared before birds in the history of life. The first known bird, *Archaeopteryx*, lived about 150 million years ago. By that time dinosaurs had already been walking the planet for about 75 million years. The similarities between birds and small meat-eating dinosaurs has led most dinosaur scientists to conclude that dinosaurs were the ancestors of birds.

Are birds the descendants of dinosaurs? This book will explore this question and guide you on an armchair expedition into the evidence linking dinosaurs and birds. It is a study filled with debate, for not all scientists agree with this idea. Along the way the book will also investigate the many kinds of dinosaurs that ruled the world and possible reasons why their time came to an abrupt end 65 million years ago.

What Is a Dinosaur?

What kind of animals were dinosaurs and how did they differ from others, including birds? Dinosaurs were reptiles, but they were a special kind that no longer exists today. Many people assume that all dinosaurs were gigantic. Some confuse them with extinct reptiles that flew (the pterosaurs) and with reptiles that lived in the sea (e.g., plesiosaurs, ichthyosaurs, and mosasaurs). How does one know for sure whether a creature was a dinosaur or not?

Dinosaurs Were Vertebrates

Dinosaurs were part of the group of animals known as vertebrates—animals with backbones. The first vertebrates were fish, followed by amphibians, reptiles, dinosaurs, and mammals and birds. The first vertebrates appeared about 520 million years ago in the form of jawless fish.[1] Dinosaurs first walked the earth about 225 million years ago, nearly 300 million years after fish had begun to populate the oceans.

Regardless of whether they live in the water, walk on the land, or fly in the air, all vertebrates share some common characteristics. The most basic common feature of all vertebrate bodies is that one side of the body is a mirror image of the other. This trait is called bilateral symmetry.

A second common feature is that the organs of vertebrates have descended from what were basically the same organs in their ancestors. This idea is called the principle of homology.

Dinosaurs shared many similar skeletal features with other vertebrates, living and extinct. Even though we rarely, if ever,

Dinosaurs, such as this *Tyrannosaurus*, were a special form of reptile.

see the actual remains of soft tissue or organs of the dinosaurs—such as the brain, heart, and gut—we can assume that dinosaurs shared most of the internal organs of today's land-dwelling vertebrates. These features allow scientists to piece together what living dinosaurs must have been like.

The Dinosaur Hip

All dinosaurs are divided into two large groups based on the structure of their hip bones. The saurischian ("lizard-hipped") group is comprised of the two-legged carnivorous theropods; the four-legged, long-necked herbivorous sauropods; and their sister group, the two-legged herbivorous prosauropods. The ornithischian ("bird-hipped") group includes all others, such as plated, armored, horned, duck-billed, and iguanodontid dinosaurs.

Both kinds of dinosaur hips allowed the hind legs to be attached underneath the body so that they could bear the entire weight of the creature. The hind legs were also connected to the hip with a ball-and-socket joint. This provided dinosaurs with increased flexibility and mobility over their reptile ancestors. The front legs were also positioned underneath the body to help bear the weight of those dinosaurs that walked on all fours.

The legs of a modern reptile, such as a crocodile or lizard, are attached to the sides of the body and do not support the full weight of the body while the creature is at rest. Reptiles lay their bellies on the ground and rise up only when they need to move. On the other hand, the position of a dinosaur was

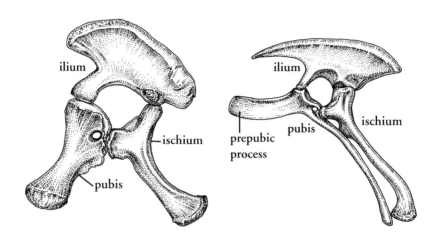

There are two kinds of dinosaur hips: saurischian ("lizard-hipped," left) and ornithiscian ("bird-hipped," right).

"always up." Dinosaurs must have been more active and energetic than today's reptiles simply because it required more stamina to hold up their body weight.

Dinosaur legs were designed more like those of mammals or birds but with some clear distinctions. While the joints in their shoulders and hips had much flexibility, those in the knees and elbows did not. This, combined with an ankle that was more like a door hinge than a ball and socket, restricted the bending of a dinosaur's forelimbs and hind limbs in one plane of motion, forward or backward. Unlike humans and other mammals, which can move sideways with ease, a dinosaur had to turn its body to face the direction it wanted to go to move to the side. They would have made lousy soccer goalies.

Dinosaurs came in many shapes and sizes. Some were many times larger than the largest land animals alive today. Others were as small as chickens. There were carnivores (they ate meat) and herbivores (they ate plants). Some dinosaurs walked on two legs, others on four. Yet, in spite of these vast differences, vertebrate paleontologists who study dinosaurs have identified many specific characteristics that allow them to classify dinosaurs as a group of related creatures, different from all others.

Dinosaurs lived only during the Mesozoic Era. The age of dinosaurs spanned from about 225 million years ago in the Late Triassic Period to the end of the Late Cretaceous Period some 65 million years ago. Fossils dating from before or after that time were not dinosaurs. This rule also means that all classic dinosaurs are *extinct.* This book will take a look at a possible descendant of the dinosaurs that is not extinct—the birds.

Dinosaurs were a special kind of reptile. Dinosaurs had basic characteristics common to all reptiles. They had a backbone and scaly skin, and they laid eggs. Some dinosaurs also showed birdlike features such as clawed feet, hollow bones, and even feathers.

Dinosaurs were land animals. Reptiles that flew in the air or lived in the water were around at the same time as dinosaurs, but they were *not* dinosaurs. Dinosaurs were

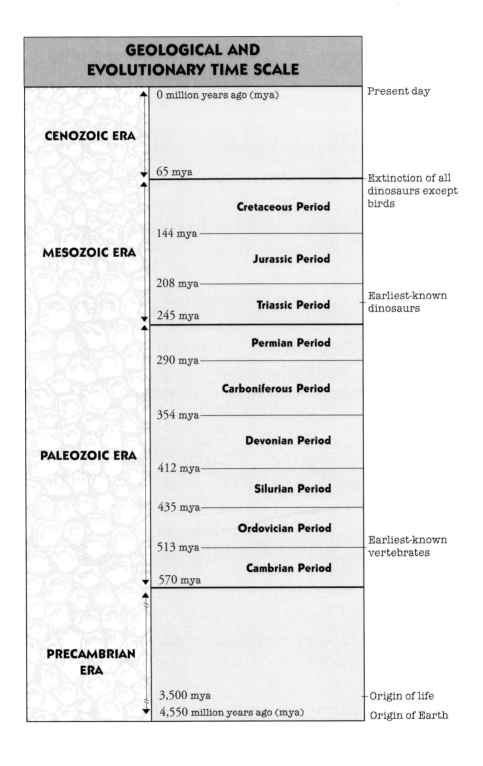

GEOLOGICAL AND EVOLUTIONARY TIME SCALE

0 million years ago (mya) — Present day

CENOZOIC ERA

65 mya — Extinction of all dinosaurs except birds

MESOZOIC ERA

Cretaceous Period

144 mya

Jurassic Period

208 mya

Triassic Period — Earliest-known dinosaurs

245 mya

Permian Period

290 mya

Carboniferous Period

354 mya

Devonian Period

PALEOZOIC ERA

412 mya

Silurian Period

435 mya

Ordovician Period

513 mya — Earliest-known vertebrates

Cambrian Period

570 mya

PRECAMBRIAN ERA

3,500 mya — Origin of life

4,550 million years ago (mya) — Origin of Earth

built to walk and live on land only, although they may have occasionally waded in the water.

Dinosaurs had special skeletal features. Dinosaurs walked differently than other reptiles because of their hips. Dinosaurs either had ornithischian ("birdlike") hips or saurischian ("lizardlike") hips. Both kinds of hips allowed dinosaurs to walk with their legs tucked under them to support their full body weight. This mammal- or birdlike stance is clearly different from the sprawling stance of today's reptiles. A dinosaur would never have dragged its stomach along the ground like a crocodile or lizard. Other distinguishing skeletal features of dinosaurs include:

- Sharp, curved teeth (in the case of a meat eater).
- Three or more vertebrae (back bones) fused together at the point where they are connected to the hip.
- A ball-and-socket joint attaching the legs to the hip for increased mobility and flexibility.
- High ankles and long foot bones. (Dinosaurs walked on their toes.)
- A simple hinge joint at the ankle.
- Three or fewer finger bones on the fourth finger of each forefoot (hand) or no fourth finger at all.
- Three to five clawed or hoofed toes on the hind limb (foot).

What Is a Bird?

Birds were the last of the five major kinds of vertebrate animals to evolve. These five kinds are fish, amphibians, reptiles,

Velociraptor is one of the most closely related dinosaurs to the dinosaur that is the common ancestor of modern birds.

mammals, and birds. It is easy to tell birds from other creatures. They have feathers and wings and most of them can fly. Today's birds are never confused with fish, lizards, mammals, and other vertebrates. People might laugh if you said that a giant dinosaur was a bird, yet dinosaurs and birds may be linked through evolution going back many, many millions of years. A number of the earliest birds were very much like small meat-eating dinosaurs. Most paleontologists now believe that birds descended from dinosaurs.

Living birds are easy to identify. The following features, which all birds share, will be good to keep in mind as we explore the relationship between dinosaurs and birds in the chapters that follow: [2]

- Toothless beak.

- A fusion of back vertebrae to form a single bony structure called the synsacrum. The synsacrum is joined to the hip bones. While dinosaurs have several fused back bones, theirs were not joined to the hip in this way.

- Wrist that allows the wing to fold tightly against the body.

- A pygostyle, or small pointed tailbone, instead of the long bony tail of a dinosaur.

- Hollow, lightweight bones.

- Two legs, like meat-eating (theropod) dinosaurs.

- A foot usually consisting of three weight-bearing toes and one small toe pointing backward, similar to theropod dinosaurs.

- A gigantic breastbone shaped like a keel, with additional surface area for the attachment of flight muscle or breast muscle.

- A wishbone, or furcula, at the point where the wings are connected to the shoulder and breast bones.

- Large brains and good eyesight that evolved to enable the complex physical movement and maneuvering required by flight.

The skeletons of the earliest birds were so similar to those of small meat-eating dinosaurs that they were sometimes confused by scientists. Two specimens of *Archaeopteryx* that lacked feather impressions were mistaken for the small dinosaur *Compsognathus* ("elegant jaw") for many years. Both were about the same size and had lightweight, hollow bones; teeth;

Archaeopteryx was the first known bird.

and the same number of claws.[3] It is no wonder that *Archaeopteryx*, with its blend of dinosaur and bird features, has been called an evolutionary link between dinosaurs and birds.

All true modern birds appeared later than both *Compsognathus* and *Archaeopteryx,* and most arrived closer to the end of the age of dinosaurs 65 million years ago. The one thing that most clearly separates birds from dinosaurs is their ability to fly. The skeletal parts needed for flight are a key difference between birds and dinosaurs.

Are Dinosaurs and Birds Related?

The meat-eating *Velociraptor* ("swift thief") and the hummingbird: How much more different could two animals be?

Not so different after all, if you listen to some dinosaur scientists. More and more fossil evidence is making it increasingly plausible that some dinosaurs were the direct ancestors of all birds.

The idea that birds and dinosaurs were close kin is almost as old as dinosaur science itself. It was first considered in 1861 by the discovery of the remarkable fossil of *Archaeopteryx* ("ancient wing"). As the earliest known bird, *Archaeopteryx* had feathers and primitive wings, as well as many of the skeletal features of small theropod (meat-eating) dinosaurs. But it was far from being a modern bird. It had teeth, and it did not have highly developed wings for powered flight. It could probably only glide from tree to tree or take off for short distances from a running start.

The similarities between meat-eating dinosaurs and birds were noted in the 1860s by dinosaur pioneers such as Edward Drinker Cope, Othniel Charles Marsh, and British naturalist Thomas Henry Huxley. Many dinosaurs are, in fact, named after the features of birds. There is even one family of dinosaurs called the Ornithomimidae ("bird mimic") because they resemble larger versions of the modern ostrich. Yet birds have several skeletal features that are generally absent from dinosaurs, including a toothless beak and wings. If some dinosaurs evolved into birds, where is the fossil evidence showing dinosaurs with more birdlike features? Without it, scientists cannot be certain whether birds sprang from dinosaurs or from some other ancestor common to them both.

The evidence is now coming to light. Since 1990, a

remarkable number of discoveries has begun to reveal clues to the evolution of dinosaurs into birds. Fifty percent of the fossil birds we currently know from the time of the dinosaurs have also been discovered since 1990.[4] This, plus the recent discovery of several remarkable birdlike dinosaurs from several continents, now leads most paleontologists to the conclusion that birds evolved from dinosaurs.

A Scientific Debate

It may be surprising to find that scientists disagree about whether dinosaurs and birds are related. This type of debate, however, is at the heart of the nature of good science.

Scientists are not always correct. Error and the correction of error are a vital part of science. When a new piece of evidence is found, it leads to more research. Over time, our understanding about a topic in science improves not only because of a new discovery, but also because of how the latest information fits with all that we have known from the past. This is especially true in paleontology, where more and better discoveries can broaden what was previously deduced from less evidence.

The theory that birds evolved from a specific group of small meat-eating dinosaurs is based on a wealth of observations and fossil evidence. While most paleontologists agree with this idea, there are some who strongly disagree. There are still some gaps in the history of these creatures that are not yet fully understood. This is the stuff of energetic scientific debate.

How can there be such a difference of opinion if we have fossil evidence? It is all a matter of how that evidence is interpreted.

The foundation of good practices in science is the *scientific method*. The scientific method is the approach used by scientists to build an accurate and reliable view of the world and nature. This is important in any science but especially in paleontology, where the evidence of past life is rare and will never be complete. The scientific method provides paleontologists with a process by which the lives of extinct creatures can be understood.

The scientific method has four basic steps. Keep these in mind as you read about the evidence in the following chapters. See if you can use the scientific method to conclude that birds evolved from dinosaurs.

Step 1. *Observation* of a phenomenon.

Step 2. Formation of a *hypothesis* to explain the phenomenon.

Step 3. Use of the hypothesis to *predict* the existence of other phenomena.

Step 4. Research to *confirm* the hypothesis.

CHAPTER 2

THE KINDS OF DINOSAURS AND WHERE THEY LIVED

When the first dinosaurs evolved, they were part of a rich biological history of life on Earth that had already spanned hundreds of millions of years.

The earliest vertebrates all lived in the water. They included lampreys, sharks, and various fish. About 370 million years ago, some ocean vertebrates adapted to breathing air and developed stronger limbs. This enabled them to leave the ocean and walk on land, at least for part of their lives. This was a monumental step in the evolution of the vertebrates.

Amphibians were one of the most successful early vertebrates to make the jump to land. But they were never able to completely separate themselves from their watery origins. Even today's amphibians begin as waterborne creatures and then take to the land as adults, returning to the water to lay and fertilize their eggs.

The most important biological event leading to true land animals was the evolution of the amniotes, vertebrate animals that could fertilize their eggs internally. This freed a creature from having to lay eggs in the water. We can thank the amphibians for being the evolutionary bridge to the first truly successful amniotes, the reptiles.

Reptiles were better suited for life on land for several reasons. Their eggs had firm or hard shells to protect them. Their limbs and other bones were sturdy enough to give them good mobility. Finally, their tough, scaly skin protected them from losing moisture. All these factors allowed reptiles to find great success on land, and they evolved into many diverse families.

Today's amniotes include reptiles and birds, which lay shelled eggs, and mammals, whose fertilized eggs develop within their bodies. Humans, birds, lizards, snakes, turtles, and even dinosaurs are all related by being amniotes.

Dinosaurs fall within the group of vertebrates known as Reptilia, or reptiles. Reptiles are egg-laying backboned animals with scaly skin. The different kinds of reptiles, living and extinct, are grouped by certain features of their skeletons. Most important is the design of the reptilian skull. Dinosaurs fall within the subclass Diapsida, which included reptiles whose skulls have a pair of openings behind each eye. Diapsida is divided into two groups: the lepidosaurs and the archosaurs. Lepidosaurs consist of the kinds of lizards and snakes that live today. Archosaurs consist of the thecodonts, a group of reptiles from the Triassic Period; the crocodiles (living and extinct); the pterosaurs (extinct flying reptiles); and the dinosaurs.[1] All dinosaurs are probably descendants of a single common archosaurian ancestor not yet identified.[2]

The dinosaurs and other diapsid reptiles were some of the most successful land vertebrates of all time. Dinosaurs first appeared about 225 million years ago and began to spread rapidly by the end of the Triassic Period.[3] Figure 1 summarizes the evolution of vertebrates leading to the dinosaurs and their bird descendents.

Dinosaur Beginnings

The archosaurs included a variety of reptiles of many sizes, some of which led to the dinosaurs. The earliest archosaurs were carnivores. Some evolved as four-legged creatures with sprawling legs, while others gradually began to walk or sprint for short distances on their two hind legs. By the Late Triassic Period, about 225 million years ago, some two-legged, meat-eating creatures had evolved specialized hips and legs to help them stand erect. This supported the full weight of their bodies while walking on two feet. They ranged in size from about 6 inches (15 centimeters) to 13 feet (4 meters). These were the archosaurs that led to the first dinosaurs.

Vertebrate Origins and Evolution
Leading to Dinosaurs

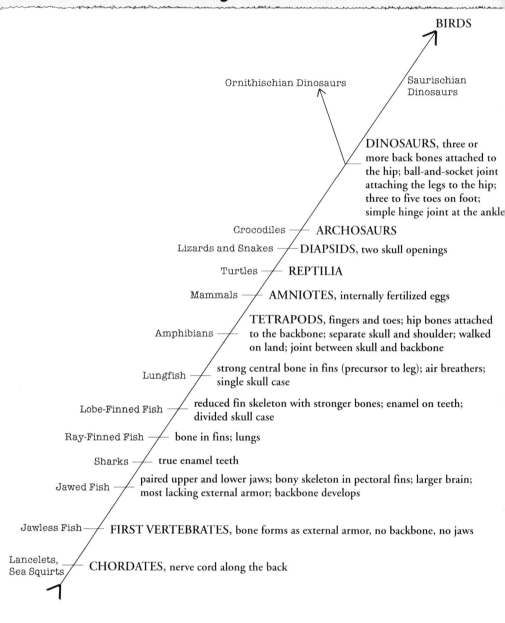

BIRDS

Ornithischian Dinosaurs

Saurischian Dinosaurs

DINOSAURS, three or more back bones attached to the hip; ball-and-socket joint attaching the legs to the hip; three to five toes on foot; simple hinge joint at the ankle

Crocodiles — **ARCHOSAURS**

Lizards and Snakes — **DIAPSIDS,** two skull openings

Turtles — **REPTILIA**

Mammals — **AMNIOTES,** internally fertilized eggs

TETRAPODS, fingers and toes; hip bones attached to the backbone; separate skull and shoulder; walked on land; joint between skull and backbone

Amphibians —

Lungfish — strong central bone in fins (precursor to leg); air breathers; single skull case

Lobe-Finned Fish — reduced fin skeleton with stronger bones; enamel on teeth; divided skull case

Ray-Finned Fish — bone in fins; lungs

Sharks — true enamel teeth

Jawed Fish — paired upper and lower jaws; bony skeleton in pectoral fins; larger brain; most lacking external armor; backbone develops

Jawless Fish — **FIRST VERTEBRATES,** bone forms as external armor, no backbone, no jaws

Lancelets, Sea Squirts — **CHORDATES,** nerve cord along the back

Figure 1. This diagram shows the evolution of vertebrate animals that resulted in the dinosaurs and birds. The steps along the way include evolutionary developments directly related to the traits of dinosaurs. The time span from the appearance of the first chordates (animals with primitive backbones) to the last dinosaur, not including birds, is about 460 million years.

Families of Dinosaurs and Their Origins

Dinosaurs came in many shapes and sizes. Some evolved from the saurischian-hipped variety, others from the ornithischian-hipped kind. Figure 2 shows the evolutionary relationships of different kinds of dinosaurs.

The Theropods. The theropods ("beast foot") were the meat-eating dinosaurs. They were the first dinosaurs to appear and among the last to become extinct during the 160-million-year reign of the dinosaurs. They evolved into several diverse kinds and sizes. They adapted some of the most advanced carnivorous weaponry ever possessed by land-dwelling creatures.

Dinosaur and Bird Evolution

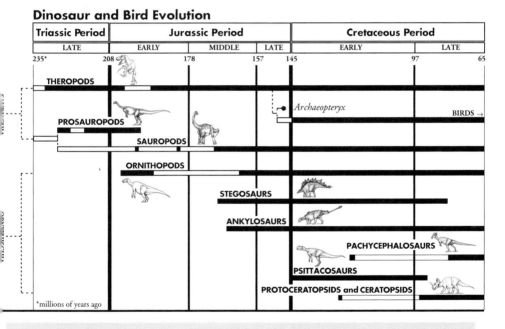

Figure 2. The evolution and groupings of all dinosaurs. Solid bars show known fossil evidence. White bars show gaps in our current knowledge. These three groups of dinosaurs were not closely related.

All theropods had one thing in common: They were designed to kill and devour other creatures. Scientists know this from studying their bones and the clues that reveal their predatory nature. All theropods walked on two legs, most had curved bladelike teeth for tearing flesh from their prey, and they were all equipped with special hand or foot claws to help them catch and kill their victims. For many scientists, the word *theropod* includes birds, so when discussing meat-eating dinosaurs, the term they use is "non-avian theropod." However, for this book, when we say *theropod*, we mean "non-avian theropod."

Eoraptor ("dawn thief"), *Herrerasaurus* ("Herrera's lizard"), and *Staurikosaurus* ("cross lizard") are the most primitive known dinosaurs. All have been found in Late Triassic deposits of South America dating from about 225 million years ago. They resembled small theropods in many ways.[4] From these distinctive beginnings spawned a remarkable lineage of theropods that menaced every generation of plant-eating dinosaurs until their demise at the end of the Cretaceous Period (65 million years ago).

The smallest known theropod is *Microraptor* ("small thief"), which was about the size of a crow.[5] Several giant meat eaters contend for the title of world heavyweight champion, including the familiar *Tyrannosaurus* ("tyrant lizard")

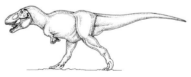

Tyrannosaurus

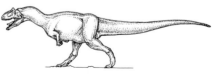

Allosaurus

from North America, as well as *Giganotosaurus* ("gigantic southern lizard") and its kin from South America, and *Carcharodontosaurus* ("sharp-toothed lizard") and *Spinosaurus* ("spiny lizard") from Africa.

While some theropods, such as *Allosaurus* ("different lizard"), *Tyrannosaurus*, *Coelophysis* ("hollow form"), and others are quite well known from fossil specimens, most

Coelophysis

are not. More than 75 percent of the known theropods are understood only from the partial remains of single individuals. This leaves many gaps in scientists' knowledge. Paleontologists do not always agree on which theropods are most closely related to each other. Our knowledge about the family tree of theropods improves every year as more specimens are discovered.

The fossils of several small, feathered theropods recently discovered in China have provided important new evidence linking the evolution of dinosaurs and birds. They include *Sinosauropteryx* ("Chinese lizard wing"), *Protarchaeopteryx* ("before Archaeopteryx"), and *Caudipteryx* ("tail feather").

The Prosauropods and Sauropods. Prosauropods and sauropods were long-necked browsing plant eaters. The most familiar sauropods are *Apatosaurus* ("deceptive lizard"), *Brachiosaurus* ("arm lizard"), *Seismosaurus* ("earth-shaker lizard"),

Brachiosaurus

and *Diplodocus* ("double beam"). This group includes the largest land creatures ever to walk

Diplodocus

the earth. The longest may have been about 150 feet (45 meters) long. The tallest could have looked over the top of a baseball stadium. The heaviest weighed between 90 and 100 tons.

Prosauropods were the first of these two families of dinosaurs to evolve. Even though they had large bodies, long necks, and small heads, they were not directly related to the sauropods that followed. The prosauropods arose during the Late Triassic Period (208 to 225 million years ago) and were

The fossils of *Sinosauropteryx* discovered in China give new evidence that links the evolution of dinosaurs and birds.

the most plentiful terrestrial plant eaters of that time. But prosauropods were completely gone by the end of the Early Jurassic Period, probably because they were pushed aside by the bigger herbivores on the block, the sauropods. The family line of prosauropods concludes at that time, an evolutionary dead end.

Sauropods arose rapidly from their roots in the Early Jurassic Period. By the Middle Jurassic Period, they had become the dominant terrestrial life-form throughout the world. But how they first evolved is unclear. Sauropods were once thought to have been descendants of the prosauropods. This seems unlikely because sauropods had certain skeletal features, such as the fifth digit of the hind foot, that had already been greatly reduced even in the earliest known prosauropods.[6] It is more likely that the prosauropods and sauropods evolved at the same time from a common ancestor but along different paths.

The bodies of these gigantic creatures were adapted to process the large quantities of vegetation needed to sustain life in such big animals. Their days were mainly spent looking for more plants to eat. Along the way, they needed to keep an eye out, or a nose out, for predatory dinosaurs that fancied them as their next meal.

Only about half of the known sauropods are known from good specimens. Paleontologists do not always agree on which sauropods are most closely related to each other. There is always hope, though, that knowledge about the genealogy of sauropods will improve greatly with new discoveries.

The Ornithopods. The ornithopods were a plentiful group of two-legged plant eaters that thrived for most of the age of dinosaurs. They filled a place in nature that is today occupied by cattle, moose, horses, antelopes, and other peaceable plant eaters and provided a steady supply of food for predators. Ornithopods were the most successful and widespread of all herbivorous dinosaurs in the Cretaceous Period. There is evidence that some traveled in great herds, nested in large colonies to lay their eggs, and possibly took care of their young until their offspring were large enough to fend for themselves. Ornithopods first walked the earth in the Early Jurassic Period, not long after the appearance of the earliest dinosaurs. The last of the great ornithopods disappeared at the end of the age of dinosaurs along with *Tyrannosaurus,* the horned dinosaurs, and the last of the armored and sauropod dinosaurs.

The term *ornithopod,* which is short for *Ornithopoda* ("bird-footed"), is a suborder of the ornithischian dinosaurs. Ornithopoda includes several kinds of dinosaurs that are much better known by other names. They include *Iguanodon* ("iguana tooth"), the second dinosaur ever described, and the hadrosaur or duck-billed

Iguanodon

dinosaurs, so named because their spoonlike mouth resembled that of a duck. Familiar duck-billed dinosaurs include *Edmontosaurus* ("Edmonton lizard"), *Corythosaurus* ("helmet lizard"), and *Parasaurolophus* ("similar crested lizard"). One family of duck-billed dinosaurs is known for the elaborate crests on top of their heads. These crests were actually part

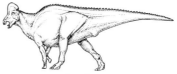

Corythosaurus

of their nose and could have been used to make sounds.

Unlike some other plant-eating dinosaurs that had armor and horns, ornithopods had few special defenses. They ranged

Heterodontosaurus

in length from about 4 feet (1.2 meters) in *Heterodontosaurus* ("different-toothed lizard") to about 49 feet (14.7 meters) for the duck-billed dinosaur *Shantungosaurus* ("Shantung lizard").

Only about 18 percent of all the individual kinds, or genera, of dinosaurs recognized so far are ornithopods. This figure may seem low, but ornithopods existed in greater numbers than most other kinds of dinosaurs. The fossil record of ornithopods is good. Many are known from nearly complete skeletons or multiple specimens as opposed to the fragmentary evidence for many kinds of sauropods and theropods. So, although we may be able to name a larger number of different kinds of meat-eating dinosaurs, the ornithopods and other plant eaters on which they fed greatly outnumbered them.

The Horned Dinosaurs. All horned dinosaurs are included in the suborder Ceratopsia. The name *Ceratopsia* means "horned face." It includes smaller, hornless varieties, such as *Psittacosaurus* ("parrot lizard") and *Protoceratops* ("first horned face"), as well as their famous horned cousins, *Triceratops* ("three-horned face"), *Styracosaurus* ("spiked lizard"), *Torosaurus* ("piercing lizard"), and *Einiosaurus* ("buffalo lizard").

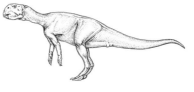

Psittacosaurus

Compared to other dinosaurs, the ceratopsians were latecomers. Their first traces go back only about 140 million years to the latter part of the Early Cretaceous Period. By the time they walked the earth, more than two thirds of the known dinosaurs had already become extinct.

Ceratopsians had ornithischian hips. They were all herbivores. An early family of Ceratopsia was the psittacosaurs.

Einiosaurus, which means "buffalo lizard," was one of the horned dinosaurs.

They were only about 6.5 feet (2 meters) long, including the tail. They weighed about as much as a German shepherd. They were primarily bipedal, walking on their long back legs. Most notable was their parrotlike beak, after which they were named. This was the forerunner of the beak seen in all ceratopsians. Like the later horned dinosaurs, psittacosaurs had cheek teeth designed for cutting tough vegetation. They also had a bony ridge around the back of the head that hinted at the large neck frill seen in other ceratopsians.

The next oldest variety of ceratopsians was the protoceratopsids. They were also small dinosaurs, and although they walked primarily on four legs, they could probably rear up or even run on their hind legs when needed.

The largest of the horned dinosaurs were the ceratopsids. Larger than the rhinoceros, they thundered along on four legs and were decorated with exquisite horns and frills.

Many of the ceratopsians are well known from abundant fossil specimens. Most dinosaurs are known from only about five specimens per kind, or genus. With horned dinosaurs, there are about nine or ten specimens per genus, and sometimes many more.[7] The fact that these creatures lived during the most recent part of the age of dinosaurs increases the likelihood that scientists will find their fossils. This is because their bones have had less time to sit in the earth and disintegrate than some of the earlier dinosaurs.

The Armored, Plated, and Bone-Headed Dinosaurs.
The armored, plated, and bone-headed dinosaurs were related by being plant eaters with ornithischian hips. Otherwise, they

were from different branches of the dinosaur family tree and not too much alike. The stegosaurs ("plated lizards") had large plates or spikes on their backs and a set of spikes at the ends of their tails. The ankylosaurs ("armored lizards") had extensive body armor, and some members of this group had large bony clubs at the ends of their tails. The pachycephalosaurs ("thick-headed lizards") had thick, rounded caps on top of their skulls that could be used to butt opponents.

The remains of armored, plated, and bone-headed dinosaurs are some of the rarest of all dinosaurs, but several excellent specimens provide clues to their nature. They lived at different times, but there was a span during the Early to Late Cretaceous Period when some members of each family walked the earth together. The armored and plated dinosaurs were bulky, four-legged creatures often measuring about 20 to 30 feet (6 to 9 meters) in length, whereas the bone-headed dinosaurs were two-legged and measured 2 to 15 feet (0.6 to 4.5 meters) long.

The plated dinosaurs, or stegosaurs, were the first of these three families to appear. The earliest stegosaur fossils have been found in China and date from the Middle Jurassic Period about 170 million years ago. Familiar stegosaurs include *Stegosaurus* ("plated lizard") and *Kentrosaurus* ("spiked lizard").

Stegosaurus

Armored dinosaurs are divided into two families according to whether they had a tail club or not. Those with clubs are of the family Ankylosauridae, and those without are from the family Nodosauridae. The Ankylosauridae first appeared at the end of the Middle Jurassic Period and were fol-

Kentrosaurus

lowed in the Late Jurassic Period by the first known nodosaurs. Both families of armored dinosaurs outlasted the stegosaurs and were still around at the end of the Late Cretaceous Period when the last of the dinosaurs became extinct. Familiar armored

Euoplocephalus

dinosaurs include *Ankylosaurus* ("armored lizard"), *Euoplocephalus* ("well-armored head"), and *Nodosaurus* ("knobby lizard").

The bone-headed dinosaurs are from a family called Pachycephalosauridae. They were the latecomers of this group. The first known member, *Yaverlandia* (after Yaverland Battery on the Isle of Wight), appeared in the Early Cretaceous Period. Most other known members of the bone-headed family are from the Late Cretaceous Period. Pachycephalosaurs are usually divided into two families based on the shape and slope of their skullcaps. Those with flatter heads are members of the family Homalocephalidae, and those with rounded, domed heads are members of the family Pachycephalosauridae.

The Geographic Range of Dinosaurs

The earth underwent dramatic geologic changes during the 160-million-year reign of the dinosaurs. When the dinosaurs

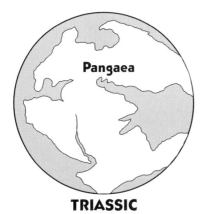

TRIASSIC

EARLY JURASSIC

EARLY CRETACEOUS

first appeared during the Late Triassic Period, the continents that we know today were still joined together as one super-continent known as Pangaea. By the end of the Mesozoic Era, when the last of the horned dinosaurs perished, the continents had gradually begun to break apart to form the major landmasses known today as North and South America, Africa, Europe, Asia, Australia, and Antarctica.

When the continents were joined, it was possible for dinosaurs to travel between the northern and the southern boundaries of dry land. This is why many of the early dinosaurs, including the theropods (meat eaters), prosauropods, sauropods (long-necked plant eaters), and early ornithopods (plant eaters), can be found on most of the continents in the Northern and Southern

Hemispheres. They spread rapidly around the globe while the continents were still connected. By the time of the horned, duck-billed, and armored dinosaurs, the Northern and Southern Hemispheres had split apart. This made migration from the Northern Hemisphere to the Southern Hemisphere impossible. Horned dinosaurs, duckbills, and iguanodonts appear to have originated in the Northern Hemisphere, probably in Asia. Their remains are rare or nonexistent in the southern continents. Although most armored, plated, and bone-headed dinosaurs have been found in the Northern Hemisphere, a few have been found in the Southern Hemisphere, including in Africa (stegosaurs and pachycephalosaurs), India (stegosaurs; India was once a part of the lower continents), Australia (nodosaur), and South America (traces of ankylosaurs). North America was still connected to Asia by a land bridge during the earlier part of the Late Cretaceous Period. This accounts for the similarities between the theropod, sauropod, ornithopod, armored, plated, and bone-headed dinosaurs found on these two continents.

The arrangement of the continents as we know them today was formed during the end of the Cretaceous Period, the end of the dinosaur era. The map on the next pages illustrates the range of dinosaur fossil locations around the world.

Geographic
all Dinosaur

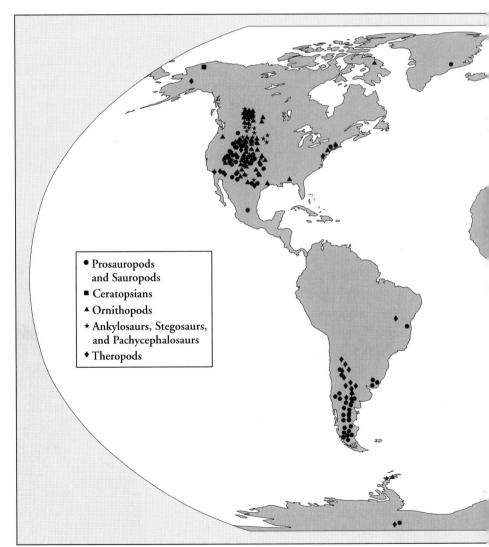

- Prosauropods
  and Sauropods
- Ceratopsians
- Ornithopods
- Ankylosaurs, Stegosaurs,
  and Pachycephalosaurs
- Theropods

Range of Families

CHAPTER 3

THE ORIGIN AND EVOLUTION OF BIRDS

Archaeopteryx is considered to be the first bird, but it was far from being like a modern bird. It had several primitive features not seen in modern birds including teeth, a long bony tail, no synsacrum, and unfused bones in its hands.[1] It had features that dismiss it as being the direct ancestor of all birds, but it remains a spectacular combination of theropod dinosaur and bird characteristics. It is difficult to name a better fossil representing evolution in the works, which is why *Archaeopteryx* is sometimes called the world's most valuable fossil.

Although valuable, *Archaeopteryx* represents only one point in time during the evolution of birds. Relying only on *Archaeopteryx* to tell the entire story of bird evolution is like trying to predict the outcome of a basketball game from one minute of play in the first quarter—many things can happen after that to affect the result. If we think of *Archaeopteryx* as having appeared in the "first quarter" of the evolution of modern birds, what other players and changes appeared along the way to affect the outcome we see today? Unfortunately, there are some big gaps in our knowledge about the evolution of birds between the appearance of *Archaeopteryx* in the Late Jurassic Period and the end of the Cretaceous Period 75 million years later. This was a critical time in the evolution of birds. By the end of the Cretaceous Period, most of the roots of modern bird families had come into being.

Knowing how birds first evolved depends on the fossils that we can collect from the time of the dinosaurs. As you might expect, the small lightweight skeletons of birds did not fossilize as easily as the larger, bulky bones of their dinosaur neighbors. Scientists often have to look longer and harder to find bird fossils. Fortunately, paleontologists have turned their attention to ancient birds with renewed enthusiasm since 1990. The result is that three times as many Cretaceous bird fossils have been found since 1990 than in all of the previous history of paleontology.[2]

During the 75 million years between *Archaeopteryx* and the end of the Cretaceous Period, the reptilian features of early birds evolved into features that make up modern birds. The long bony tail, long legs, teeth, and clawed fingers of *Archaeopteryx* were an obvious testament to its reptilian ancestry. In the modern flying birds that followed, the body became more compact and short and the center of gravity moved forward from that seen in *Archaeopteryx* and bipedal theropod dinosaurs. The center of gravity in bipedal dinosaurs was over the hips to keep them balanced when they ran. In modern flying birds, the center of gravity is forward of the hips and lined up with the wings to keep them balanced while flying. Modern flying birds also have a stump known as the pygostyle instead of a tail, have no teeth, and their breastbone was transformed into a broad, keeled sternum for the attachment of flight muscles.

By the end of the Cretaceous Period, no fewer than fourteen branches of the bird family tree had been rooted. Of these, eight went on to flourish as modern birds past the end of the Cretaceous. The history of these bird groups is only represented by sketchy fossil evidence. However, a number of important finds since 1990 are beginning to fill in the gaps in our knowledge:

Sinornis ("Chinese bird"). Dating from about 135 million years ago in China, *Sinornis* is one of the earliest known birds to have shed many of its reptilian features. Living only about 10 million years after *Archaeopteryx,* its shortened body, pygostyle (rather than a tail), and folding wings made its body plan closer to that of a modern bird. But it still had the teeth, clawed fingers, and small breastbone seen in *Archaeopteryx.*

Confuciusornis ("Confucius' bird"). This Early Cretaceous bird dates from the same time as the famous feathered dinosaurs (which you will read about in Chapter 4) and was also found in Liaoning, China. It had a body like that of *Archaeopteryx* but a skull like that of a modern bird.

Eoalulavis ("early little wing bird"). This bird lived in what is now Spain about 115 million years ago in the Early Cretaceous Period. It included many anatomical improvements for flight over the primitive flyer Archaeopteryx. Most notably, it had the oldest known alula, a group of feathers on the front edge of the bird's wing that helped sustain lift as the bird flew slowly.

Rahonavis ("menace from the clouds bird"). This bird had a 2-foot (0.6-meter) wingspan, lived in Madagascar during the Late Cretaceous, and had a threatening sickle claw on the second toe of each foot, just like dromaeosaur dinosaurs.

The Evolution of Flight

Powered flight is not unique to birds. Insects and bats can fly under their own power; pterosaurs (extinct flying reptiles) could also. Among animals with backbones, powered flight has evolved three separate times—first in pterosaurs, then in birds, and finally in bats—each independent of one another. This is called convergent evolution and means that different kinds of animals, although otherwise unrelated, adapted to their environment by evolving similar anatomical features.

There are three anatomical requirements for flight that are shared by bats, pterosaurs, and birds:

- Lightweight body—Hollow bones and sometimes fewer bones in the back.

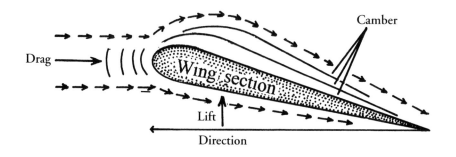

When viewed in cross-section, the curved upper surface of a wing is longer than its flat lower surface. Air moving over the top of the surface must travel farther and faster than the air moving underneath. The difference forces the body upward.

- Airfoil to produce lift—The wing is an airfoil. When combined with forward motion, it produces lift, the force that allows a body to become airborne.

- Energy to take off—Most modern birds are strong enough to become airborne from a standing start. Just how the earliest birds launched themselves is an active debate.

Archaeopteryx may be the earliest known bird, but it tells us little about the evolution of bird flight. It is clear from the design of its wings and feathers that *Archaeopteryx* could fly to some degree. But it lacked many of the special adaptations of modern birds that make them excellent flyers. It still had a tail and a long body. Its breast and shoulder bones were not big enough for the attachment of large and strong flight muscles. Its wrists and hands were still more suited for grasping and climbing than for being part of a well-adapted and powerful wing.[3] For these reasons, *Archaeopteryx* is more like a snapshot in time between the origins of bird flight and the powered flight of modern birds than an answer to the puzzle of how birds began to fly.

Taking Wing From the Ground or a Tree— Which Was First?

How did the earliest birds ever get off the ground? This question has been waiting for an explanation since the early days of paleontology.

Because there is no solid evidence of feathered, flying creatures prior to *Archaeopteryx*, two theories have been offered for the beginnings of bird flight. One theory assumes that bird flight began as a "trees-down" phenomenon, probably with creatures that could glide from a tree to the ground before they evolved powered flight. The other theory assumes a "ground-up" origin, where small running dinosaurs gradually adapted their leaping and maneuvering into flapping flight.

The trees-down theory is attractive because it assumes that gliding was possible in these creatures before they could fly on their own power. One can easily imagine an early bird gliding or parachuting down from a tree branch. It simply makes sense. As they became more skilled at gliding, turning their bodies and wings to steer themselves and control their fall, they began to build the physical adaptations that evolved into powered flight. Perching in a tree would have been an early feature. If this is true, and if dinosaurs were the ancestors of birds, why and when did dinosaurs start to climb trees? The answer is that many scientists who support the trees-down theory think that something other than a dinosaur led to the first birds. A likely candidate is a four-legged archosaur, an early reptile and part of the same group of reptiles from which the earliest dinosaurs evolved.

The ground-up theory is more challenging to picture, but it fits with the many similarities observed in the skeletons of small meat-eating dinosaurs and early birds. In this theory, small dinosaurs began to leap and improve their maneuverability while running along the ground. Running, dodging, and leaping would have been important for catching food and also for escaping from other predators. The animal may have become briefly airborne while doing this. The act of reaching forward with both hands to grasp a prey might have led to the flapping motion seen later in powered flight. Over millions of years, the arms of some theropod dinosaurs may have gradually changed into wings as the design of their arms became more and more specialized. *Archaeopteryx* seems to be a creature that evolved from the ground up, for it still has the legs, feet, and hands of its ground-dwelling dinosaur ancestor.

Feathers Will Not Always Fly

One of the most familiar features of birds is feathers. Although feathers aid in flight, they are not necessary for the development of powered flight. Bats and pterosaurs both achieved powered flight without having feathers, their wings being covered with a thin membrane of skin.

Until the recent discovery of flightless but feathered

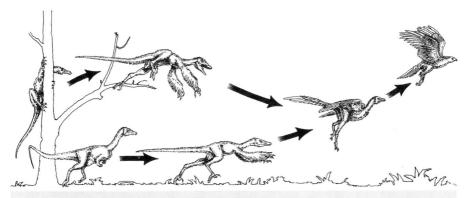

In the trees-down theory of flight origin, a four-legged tree-dwelling archosaur begins as a gliding reptile and evolves into a bird with powered flight. In the ground-up theory of flight origin, running dinosaurs evolve wings over time due to the elongation and flapping motion of their arms.

dinosaurs, it was thought that feathers must have evolved along with the first birds. It now seems that feathers existed on some kinds of small meat-eating dinosaurs before the evolution of birds. The feathers probably served the purpose of insulating the dinosaur from hot and cold temperatures and were not directly related to flight at first.[4] Gradually the arms of certain dinosaurs became more winglike. Feathers once used solely for insulation evolved to give them more maneuverability and to create the airfoil needed first for gliding and then for powered flight.

One thing still seems clear. Feathers have such a unique structure that they probably evolved only once. Birds and dinosaurs are the only creatures known to have had feathers. Until other fossil evidence is found that might prove otherwise, the presence of feathers is a compelling reason to believe that birds evolved from small feathered dinosaurs.

CHAPTER 4

FEATHERED DINOSAURS

Until just a few years ago, the only known creatures that had feathers were birds. With feathers also came wings, even in the case of flightless birds such as the penguin. This held true for all known extinct creatures as well as those that are alive today. Even *Archaeopteryx*, despite resembling dinosaurs in many ways, was considered to be a bird because it had wings and feathers.

A discovery in northeast China in 1996 changed all that. Found in rocks dating from about 125 million years ago, in the Early Cretaceous Period, the well-preserved specimen of a small meat-eating dinosaur revealed that something fuzzy had been covering its neck, back, and other parts of its body. The bones were encased in a fine-grained slab of mudstone and showed the dinosaur lying flat on its side in a death pose. The fuzz appeared as a dark halo around the outline of the skeleton. Some scientists interpreted the fuzz as down, the fluffy coating that young birds have prior to growing feathers.[1] Michael William Skrepnick, the illustrator of this book series, was fortunate enough to be in China when this specimen was first shown to Canadian dinosaur expert Philip J. Currie. Michael's sketch of this fuzzy dinosaur as it might have appeared in life became the world's first view of what has now become one of the most important fossil discoveries of the twentieth century.[2]

The skeleton of this small dinosaur was remarkably well preserved in much the same manner as the famous *Archaeopteryx*. The tiniest of details were preserved. The dinosaur measured only 3.3 feet (1 meter) long and was complete except for the tip of its tail. Meat-eating teeth were clearly preserved in its jaws. It had dinosaurlike limbs and arms. A close-up look at the downy coat on its back revealed that the down consisted of short strandlike filaments. A team of leading Chinese and western paleontologists, including bird and dinosaur experts, worked together to

This was the first impression of *Sinosauropteryx* seen by the world. It was made by Michael William Skrepnick while visiting China in 1996, one month after the specimen was first discovered.

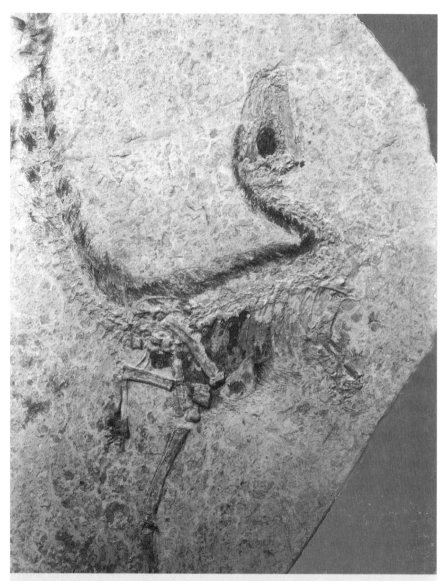

Bird or dinosaur? *Sinosauropteryx* was about 3.3 feet (1 meter) long. It closely resembled a small meat-eating dinosaur. Note, however, that it had a fuzzy covering stretching from its head to its tail. These "protofeathers" were interpreted as a form of down or featherlike coat.

decipher the mystery of the downy dinosaur. They examined the specimen under the microscope and pooled their collective wisdom to interpret this spectacular creature. While they could not fully agree on the nature of the downy covering, they all agreed that the fuzz was not feathers. Some called it protofeathers, but its precise nature and purpose is a point of debate among paleontologists. Some scientists believe that protofeathers were a possible stage in the early evolution of feathers that had not been seen before.[3] They were clearly a decoration of some kind on the animal, but whether they were composed of keratin, like a feather or claw, or collagen, like skin, is not yet at all clear.

The new dinosaur was named *Sinosauropteryx* ("Chinese lizard wing") by Chinese scientists. Originally thinking that it was a primitive bird, they named it after *Archaeopteryx*. *Sinosauropteryx* is now considered to be a dinosaur and not a bird, mostly because it has no wings. Renowned paleontologist John Ostrom of Yale University was a member of a scientific team that took a close look at *Sinosauropteryx*. He remarked that the Chinese fossil is strikingly similar to that of *Compsognathus*, a chicken-sized dinosaur dating from the Late Jurassic Period of Germany and France. Both had long necks, short arms, and long legs.

Sinosauropteryx was found in an ancient lake-bed deposit in the Liaoning Province of China. Since its discovery, many other unusual specimens of ancient birds, dinosaurs, fish, turtles, and other creatures from that time have been found in the Liaoning area. It is one of the richest fossil regions in all the world for the study of Early Cretaceous dinosaurs, birds, plants, insects, mammals, and other creatures. The fossil deposits are so rich and the specimens so complete that they leave little to imagine. A wealth of detail about these wonderful creatures is revealed by their exquisitely preserved skeletons. The world's oldest complete mammal fossil—*Jeholodens* ("tooth of Jehol")—was found there, giving us a look at a rat-sized creature that lived in the shadow of the feathered dinosaurs. The oldest known flowering plant was also discovered in the formation. Life was teeming in and around the ancient lake.

More Fuzz and Feathers

A little over a year after the naming of *Sinosauropteryx*, two more remarkable little dinosaurs were discovered in the same region of China. This time, however, the remains included the distinct impressions of feathers. This was the first unquestionable discovery of *flightless feathered dinosaurs*. They lived at the same time as *Sinosauropteryx*.

The first of the two dinosaurs was *Protarchaeopteryx* ("before *Archaeopteryx*"). It is so named because if birds evolved from dinosaurs, it is considered to be the theropod dinosaur most closely related to the earliest known bird, *Archaeopteryx*. The second dinosaur was *Caudipteryx* ("tail feather"). *Caudipteryx* was almost 3 feet (1 meter) long, a little bigger than *Protarchaeopteryx*. Both had teeth, hands and claws like theropods, and well-preserved feathers in the breast and tail areas. The specimen of *Protarchaeopteryx* also includes some scraps of the fuzzy filaments or down first seen in *Sinosauropteryx*, lending credence to the idea that the fuzz was related to early feathers.

Although both of these dinosaurs had feathers, they did not have well-developed wings and could not fly even as well as the poor-flying *Archaeopteryx*. They were both ground-dwelling animals and may represent one of two possibilities in the evolution of dinosaurs and birds. Scientists who believe that birds descended from dinosaurs view *Protarchaeopteryx* and *Caudipteryx* as stages in the evolution of birds from two-legged, feathered dinosaurs. However, at least one team of scientists casts doubt on this conclusion by suggesting that the center of mass in *Protarchaeopteryx* and *Caudipteryx* was more forward than in theropod dinosaurs, but similar to that seen in flightless birds.[4] They suggest that rather than being the

The first known cases of unambiguously feathered dinosaurs were *Protarcheaopteryx* and *Caudipteryx*. Pictured here is *Caudipteryx*.

descendants of dinosaurs, these creatures may have been flightless birds descended from birds after the origin of *Archaeopteryx*. If, however, these two feathered creatures prove to be dinosaurs, the fact that they did not fly also means that feathers and flight evolved independently. In the case of these creatures, feathers were probably used for insulation.[5]

Another small Chinese theropod dinosaur with traces of featherlike filaments was discovered in 1999. It, too, came from the Liaoning Province in northeastern China. Named *Beipiaosaurus* ("Beipiao lizard") after the city near which it was found, it is a strangely primitive creature that resembles in part the dromaeosaurs and also the little-known therizinosaurs. Therizinosaurs were unusual meat-eating dinosaurs in that they had long arms and claws, and although

Beipiaosaurus was a therizinosaurid dinosaur with feathers.

they were considered meat eaters, their teeth may have also been suited to eating plants.

Beipiaosaurus shows traces of featherlike filaments similar to those found in *Sinosauropteryx.* These filaments or protofeathers can be seen around the arms, legs, and shoulders.[6]

Following the first discovery of the feathered dinosaurs came several other significant finds linking birds to dinosaurs. The same locality in China that yielded the feathered dinosaurs also revealed an early dromaeosaurid dinosaur that had filaments or protofeathers. The new downy dinosaur, named *Sinornithosaurus* ("Chinese bird lizard") had a fuzzy coating, including fibers on its arms.[7] As a member of the family of dinosaurs known as Dromaeosauridae, this new dinosaur is part of a group that includes the small, vicious raptors of movie fame. Each had a deadly sickle claw on the second toe of each foot. Other members of this family included *Deinonychus* ("ter-rible claw"), *Velociraptor* ("swift thief"), and *Dromaeosaurus* ("swift lizard"). This relationship is

Deinonychus

significant because *Velociraptor* and its relatives have been identified by paleontologists as one of the branches of the dinosaur family tree most closely related to birds.

Further cementing this link to dromaesaurs was yet another remarkable dinosaur revealed in April 2001. A joint team from China and America described a small theropod

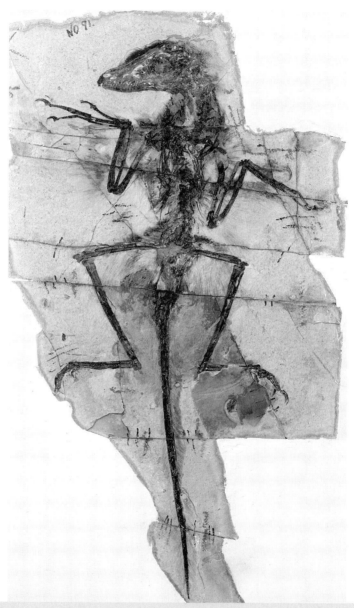

This duck-sized dinosaur discovered in China in 2000 was covered with primitive feathers and dinosaur fuzz from head to tail. It provides excellent evidence that dinosaurs had feathers for warmth and insulation before the evolution of flight.

discovered in the Liaoning region of China that was covered with primitive feathers from head to tail.[8] The small dinosaur, whose entire fossilized skeleton was present, offered further evidence that dinosaurs developed feathers for warmth and insulation prior to the evolution of flight in birds. This small meat eater was about the size of a duck and dates from the Early Cretaceous Period. It was a dromaeosaur like *Sinornithosaurus.*

CHAPTER 5

ARE BIRDS DESCENDED FROM DINOSAURS?

Demonstrating with certainty that birds evolved from dinosaurs may require startling fossil evidence reaching back to the Early and Middle Jurassic Periods, before the time of *Archaeopteryx*. Until such evidence is discovered—if it ever is—there are two competing hypotheses explaining the origin of birds:

1. Birds evolved from small meat-eating dinosaurs that first appeared in the Early to Middle Jurassic Period, prior to Archaeopteryx. Feathers appeared on dinosaurs as a form of decoration and possible body insulation prior to the development of wings and flight.

2. Birds did not evolve from dinosaurs but from an early archosaurian (reptilian) ancestor common to both birds and dinosaurs. This ancestor lived in the Early to Middle Jurassic Period, prior to *Archaeopteryx*. Dinosaurs and birds retained feathers from this common ancestor.

The Dinosaur-Bird Link

The recent discovery of feathered dinosaurs in China clearly shows that some small dinosaurs had feathers even though they could not fly. What does this evidence mean? Can we now say for sure that today's birds are actually direct descendants of the spectacular dinosaurs that once ruled the earth? If so, which dinosaurs were the closest relatives of birds?

Paleontologist John Ostrom ignited the modern debate over the origins of birds in 1969 with the compelling discovery of the theropod *Deinonychus*. This dinosaur was a member of the family of theropods known as Dromaeosauridae. Ostrom was struck by the similarities between this new dinosaur and *Archaeopteryx*. As a bird with reptilian features, *Archaeopteryx* was a good place to continue his investigation of the link between dinosaurs and birds. He made a detailed study of *Archaeopteryx* and described its many similarities to the dromaeosaur dinosaurs.

It was Ostrom's conclusion that dromaeosaurs and *Archaeopteryx* both evolved from a common ancestor, possibly a small, bipedal, predatory dinosaur from the Early to Middle Jurassic Period. By the time of *Archaeopteryx* in the Late Jurassic Period, early birds had begun to evolve separately from their non-flying theropod relatives, the dromaeosaurs. Whether *Archaeopteryx* was an important link in this chain or merely an evolutionary dead end has yet to be proven with certainty.

The recent discovery of small feathered theropod dinosaurs in China has given paleontologists additional support

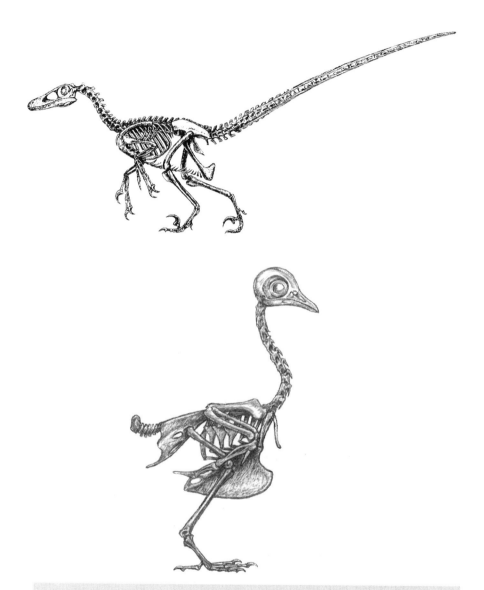

There are similarities in the anatomy of the dinosaur *Velociraptor* and a modern bird, the pigeon. They include long curved necks, two-legged posture, clawed feet, hollow bones, and arms.

for the link between dinosaurs and birds. In addition to the dramaeosaurs, several other kinds of small meat-eating dinosaurs have shown up with a mosaic of dinosaur and bird-like features. Evidence now suggests that four branches of the dinosaur family tree were closely related to the origin of birds. There were the dromaeosaurs such as *Velociraptor* and *Deinonychus*, the oviraptors such as *Oviraptor*, the troodontids such as *Troodon* ("wounding tooth"), and the strange therizinosaurs such as *Beipiaosaurus*. These dinosaurs were all small meat eaters measuring no more than 12 feet (3.6 meters) long, with some as small as 5 or 6 feet (1.5 or 2 meters) long. Some other dinosaurs, such as *Unenlagia* ("half bird") from Argentina and the flightless bird *Mononykus* ("one claw") from Mongolia, are clearly related to the link between dinosaurs and birds but do not yet fit neatly into any well-known dinosaur or bird family. There are wide gaps in the fossil evidence that need to be filled. Each of these kinds of theropod dinosaurs were small, lightweight meat eaters with skeletal features that might have led to the specialized limbs of bird wings, toothless beaks, and the lightweight, two-legged frames of true birds.

The Size Question

Another puzzle in the link between dinosaurs and birds is body size. Dinosaurs that have been linked to bird origins thus far have been much larger than birds discovered from the Mesozoic Era. Since we would expect birds to have evolved from dinosaurian forerunners of equal or smaller size, where are these ancestors of birds? There must have been some that were about the same size or smaller than the first bird, *Archaeopteryx*. Although the lack of evidence does not make a hypothesis incorrect, this size question has been the subject of criticism from those who oppose the idea of a dinosaur-bird link.

Small meat-eating dinosaurs are not actually unheard of— both *Parvicursor* ("small runner") and *Compsognathus* were about the same size as *Archaeopteryx*. But the exciting discovery in 2000 of a small meat eater with feathers added an important piece to the puzzle. *Microraptor* was a little meat-eating dinosaur from the Early Cretaceous fossil beds of Liaoning, China. At a mere 19 inches (0.5 meter) long, it was described by Chinese paleontologists as being smaller than *Archaeopteryx* and having a number of birdlike features including its hip, back bones, feather impressions preserved around its lower limbs, and foot claws similar to those of tree-dwelling birds.[1] It had a tail and arms instead of wings, and the Chinese scientists who studied it believe that it was most closely related to the dromaeosaur dinosaurs. Even though it lived about 20 million years after *Archaeopteryx*, *Microraptor* showed that small dinosaurs with many similarities to birds did exist. Some scientists feel that *Microraptor* is so birdlike that it is more closely related to *Archaeopteryx* than dromaeosaurs, having already crossed the line from being a dinosaur to being a bird.

Additional Fossil Evidence

Because the fossil record for birds is so sketchy, we must be content with whatever evidence comes up that may shed light on their origins. A number of recent, unrelated discoveries of dinosaur skeletons have revealed many birdlike surprises. Considered individually, they only give us a peek at brief moments in the evolution of dinosaurs. When viewed as a whole, they reveal a pattern of changes in various kinds of dinosaurs that link dinosaur and bird anatomy.

The first known dinosaur with a pygostyle (tailbone)— *Nomingia* ("from the Nomingiin," which is part of the Gobi Desert in Mongolia)—was revealed in June 2000.[2] The pygostyle is the tailbone that had previously been found only in birds.

Nomingia

A specimen of *Velociraptor* also joined the ranks of several known dinosaurs that had a birdlike wishbone.[3] In addition, a 7-foot- (2.1-meter-) long meat eater from Argentina named *Unenlagia* had arms that could fold close to its body much like the wings of a bird. *Sinornithosaurus* was noted for being a dromaeosaur with a downy coating, but it also had adaptations in its shoulders that could have led to the evolution of powered flight. Both of these specimens suggest how the evolution of wings could have come from changes in the arms of ground-dwelling theropod dinosaurs.[4]

Just as dinosaurs are sometimes discovered with birdlike

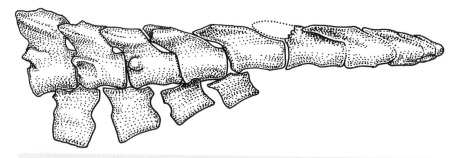

Nomingia is the first known example of a dinosaur with a pygostyle (tailbone). The pygostyle is the short tailbone that had previously only been found in birds.

features, so, too, are fossil birds being discovered with dinosaurlike features. For scientists who believe that birds descended from dinosaurs, this kind of evidence reveals the important transition period during which early birds and the dinosaurs from which they evolved shared many features.

An excellent example of a fossil bird with dinosaur features is the marvelous *Rahonavis*. This modestly large flyer had a 2-foot (0.6-meter) wingspan and lived during the Late Cretaceous Period in Madagascar off the coast of Africa. Although clearly a bird with wings and feathers, it also had a threatening sickle claw on the second toe of each foot, just like dromaeosaur dinosaurs.[5] The sickle claw suggests that this feature was retained by *Rahonavis* from its theropod dinosaur ancestors.

Similarities Between Dinosaurs and Birds

The evidence that birds descended from dinosaurs is strong. There is more than a superficial resemblance between dinosaurs and birds. The fossil discoveries described in these pages have allowed scientists to identify over 120 anatomical features that are found in small meat-eating dinosaurs and birds.[6] These include:

- Lightweight skeletons with hollow bones.

- A furcula, or wishbone, in some of the most birdlike dinosaurs, including the oviraptors *Ingenia* ("from Ingeni-Khobur"), *Oviraptor* ("egg thief"),[7] and the dromaeosaur *Bambiraptor* ("Bambi thief").[8]

- Teeth like their dinosaur ancestors in some early birds, including *Archaeopteryx*.

- A pygostyle in some birdlike dinosaurs, including oviraptorids.[9]

The bird *Rahonavis* from Madagascar had a sickle claw on its foot just like a dramaeosaur dinosaur.

- Two legs with three weight-bearing toes, on which theropod dinosaurs and birds walked.

- Dinosaur claws on birds, such as *Rahonavis*, a bird from the Late Cretaceous Period that has a sickle claw on the second toe of each foot like the dinosaur *Velociraptor*.

- Birdlike shoulder and breast bones in some dinosaurs that allow the arms to fold and move as primitive wings. This evidence is most pronounced in the small meat-eating dinosaurs *Unenlagia*[10] from South America and *Bambiraptor*[11] from Montana.

- Longer and longer arms in small theropods comparable in length to the bones of bird wings. The dromaeosaurs, which lived at the same time as known early birds following *Archaeopteryx*, had relatively long arms compared to other theropod dinosaurs.

- A growing brain capacity. We know that the relative size of the brain in a bird is greater than that found in most dinosaurs. Whereas *Tyrannosaurus* and other giant predators of the dinosaur age had a relatively small brain, the branch of meat-eating dinosaurs most closely related to birds was growing in its brain capacity as it neared the time that birds emerged. This is further evidence that birds evolved from certain kinds of dinosaurs.[12]

- Dinosaurs and birds both laid eggs. The recent discovery of an oviraptorid dinosaur fossil that was protecting a nest of eggs provides direct evidence that dinosaurs and birds shared this behavior.

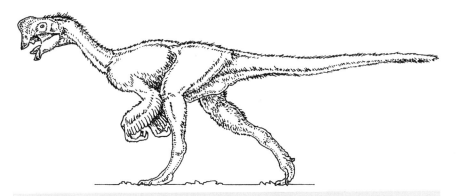

There are more than one hundred twenty anatomical features shared by dinosaurs and birds. Among these features is a wishbone, which the bird-like dinosaur, *Oviraptor*, has.

Ruffling the Feathers of Dinosaur Experts

While the idea that birds descended from dinosaurs is accepted by most paleontologists, it is not accepted by all, especially those who specialize in fossil birds. This idea remains only a hypothesis until it can be demonstrated to everyone's satisfaction.

As noted earlier, scientists who oppose the idea that birds descended from dinosaurs suggest that birds arose from another form of early reptile, as yet to be found. Here are several reasons why they believe in another theory of bird origins.

Timing Is Everything

Alan Feduccia of the University of North Carolina at Chapel Hill is one of the most vocal critics of the dinosaur-bird link. He begins with a simple argument: How could a dinosaur such as *Deinonychus* be considered part of a group that gave rise to birds, which, as shown by *Archaeopteryx* and other early birds, were already quite diverse 20 million years earlier? If *Archaeopteryx* was truly part of the family tree that led from dinosaurs to birds, where are the dinosaurs prior to *Archaeopteryx* that show that this early bird was related to dinosaurs? No clear fossil proof from before the time of *Archaeopteryx* has been found so far. However, the absence of evidence—especially in paleontology, where fossil evidence can be extremely rare—does not mean that something is not true. But it does leave the door open to alternative theories about the origin of birds.

Even the spectacular Chinese feathered dinosaurs, which appear to be a mosaic of dinosaur and birdlike features, are not immune to the argument of timing. It would be much simpler if one could conclude from the current evidence that feathers evolved on non-flying dinosaurs before they appeared on birds. But the feathered dinosaur specimens from Liaoning date from the Early Cretaceous, about 20 million years *after* the appearance of the first bird *Archaeopteryx*. So, even though these dinosaurs appear to be more primitive than *Archaeopteryx*, they actually existed much later in time. The timing of these specimens only clouds the issue until another lucky fossil hunter discovers early theropod specimens with birdlike features from before the time of *Archaeopteryx*.

The Chinese feathered dinosaurs are at the core of the timing debate. For example, *Protarchaeopteryx* and *Caudipteryx* lived between 20 and 30 million years after *Archaeopteryx*, yet

Timeline of Feathered Dinosaurs and Birds

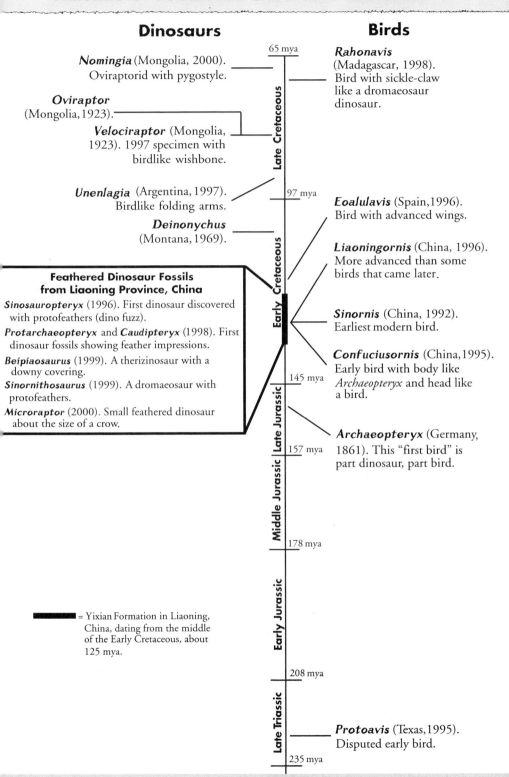

Dinosaurs

Nomingia (Mongolia, 2000). Oviraptorid with pygostyle.

Oviraptor (Mongolia, 1923).

Velociraptor (Mongolia, 1923). 1997 specimen with birdlike wishbone.

Unenlagia (Argentina, 1997). Birdlike folding arms.

Deinonychus (Montana, 1969).

Feathered Dinosaur Fossils from Liaoning Province, China

Sinosauropteryx (1996). First dinosaur discovered with protofeathers (dino fuzz).

Protarchaeopteryx and *Caudipteryx* (1998). First dinosaur fossils showing feather impressions.

Beipiaosaurus (1999). A therizinosaur with a downy covering.

Sinornithosaurus (1999). A dromaeosaur with protofeathers.

Microraptor (2000). Small feathered dinosaur about the size of a crow.

= Yixian Formation in Liaoning, China, dating from the middle of the Early Cretaceous, about 125 mya.

Birds

Rahonavis (Madagascar, 1998). Bird with sickle-claw like a dromaeosaur dinosaur.

Eoalulavis (Spain, 1996). Bird with advanced wings.

Liaoningornis (China, 1996). More advanced than some birds that came later.

Sinornis (China, 1992). Earliest modern bird.

Confuciusornis (China, 1995). Early bird with body like *Archaeopteryx* and head like a bird.

Archaeopteryx (Germany, 1861). This "first bird" is part dinosaur, part bird.

Protoavis (Texas, 1995). Disputed early bird.

Timeline labels: 65 mya, Late Cretaceous, 97 mya, Early Cretaceous, 145 mya, Late Jurassic, 157 mya, Middle Jurassic, 178 mya, Early Jurassic, 208 mya, Late Triassic, 235 mya

Evidence for the evolution of birds during the Mesozoic Period.

these two dinosaurs are more primitive in some ways than the famous first bird. Scientists who favor the link between dinosaurs and birds view these creatures as remnants of a stage in evolution prior to *Archaeopteryx*. During this time, they believe, ground-dwelling dinosaurs began to sprout feathers for insulation and their arms began to make the slow transformation into wings. *Archaeopteryx* may have risen from the same early ancestors as *Protarchaeopteryx* and *Caudipteryx*, but apparently went up a different branch that led more directly to birds. Or, it may be that modern birds as we know them sprang forth from yet another side branch of these early feathered dinosaurs that is yet unknown.

Some of the scientists who oppose the link between dinosaurs and birds suggest that a feathered dinosaur such as *Caudipteryx* is actually a flightless bird (rather than a feathered non-flying dinosaur) descended from non-dinosaurian ancestors.

Which side is correct? We cannot say for sure, because an early missing link from before the time of *Archaeopteryx* has not been found.

Evidence of Feathers Prior to *Archaeopteryx*

The origin of feathers is tightly bound to the origin of feathered dinosaurs and birds because it is generally accepted that a highly specialized structure like a feather evolved only once. Therefore, any creature older than *Archaeopteryx* that had feathers would be considered an ancestor of birds.

There is no unquestionable evidence of feathers existing

before *Archaeopteryx*, although one little creature hiding out in a Russian museum for the last thirty years has become the center of a recent controversy. *Longisquama* ("long scale") is a small reptilian creature about the size of a gerbil. It lived during the Late Triassic Period around the time the dinosaurs were first appearing. This creature was originally discovered in Central Asia and described by Russian scientists in 1970. What made it so curious was that it had six to eight pairs of plumelike projections on its back. The idea that these projections could have been related to feathers was originally dismissed many years ago. However, a recent reexamination of the specimen by a team consisting of several bird paleontologists concluded that the structures were indeed the earliest known feathers. Because *Longisquama* is clearly not a dinosaur and is also much older than *Archaeopteryx*, the scientists said that this is additional proof that the true origin of birds was not dinosaurs.[13]

Most dinosaur paleontologists strongly objected to this conclusion, and a second team reexamined the *Longisquama* fossil. This team concluded that the structures were not feathers. Instead, they agreed with earlier interpretations that *Longisquama* was decorated with thick, elongated scales.[14] *Longisquama* itself remains a puzzle rather than being an answer to the question of bird origins.

Protoavis: The First Bird?

Another fossil specimen that has caused considerable controversy is *Protoavis* ("first bird"). It was described by

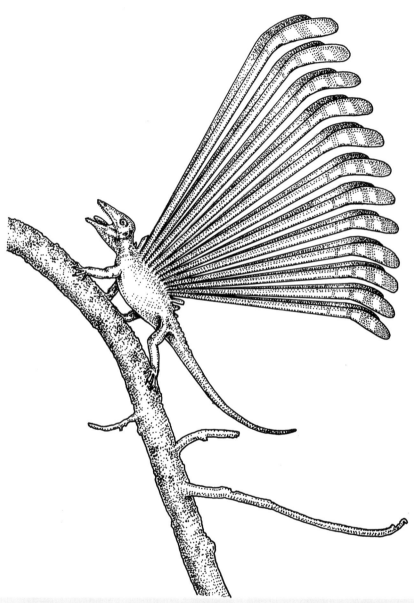

A small group of paleontologists believes that the plumelike appendages on the back of the small reptile *Longisquama* were the first feathers. This would make *Longisquama* an early ancestor of birds. Other scientists believe that the structures were elongated scales.

paleontologist Sankar Chatterjee in 1991. It dates from the Late Triassic Period of Texas. Chatterjee interpreted the fragmentary specimen as a bird, which would make it older than *Archaeopteryx* by more than 50 million years.[15] This would be an astounding revelation if everyone could agree. But other scientists who examined the fossil material did not concur with Chatterjee. Many thought that *Protoavis* consisted of the parts of several different creatures, some of which may have been theropod dinosaur in origin.[16] To this day, Chatterjee stands by his original interpretation that *Protoavis* is the first known bird, so scientists can only hope that additional fossil evidence will one day enlighten them further about the true nature of this creature. It is also interesting to note that Chatterjee believes that birds evolved from theropod dinosaurs, but he moves the transition back to nearly the origin of theropods in the Late Triassic Period.

Who Is Correct?

In Chapter 1 it was explained that the scientific method is used by scientists to prove their theories and settle debates. What conclusion does the scientific method draw about the link between birds and dinosaurs? Here is how the four steps of the scientific method can be used to understand the questions surrounding the origin of birds.

Step 1. *Observation* of a phenomenon. Many paleontologists have observed that the skeletons of birds and meat-eating dinosaurs have many similarities: over 120, in fact.

Step 2. Formation of a *hypothesis* to explain the phenomenon. A hypothesis was formed stating that birds evolved from certain kinds of dinosaurs. The most likely ancestors of birds, based on similarities in skeletal features, were the dromaeosaurs, oviraptors, and therizinosaurs—all small meat-eating dinosaurs.

Step 3. Use of the hypothesis to *predict* the existence of other phenomena. If dinosaurs were the ancestors of birds, there could be fossil evidence showing some of the stages of change in dinosaurs that led to the evolution of the first birds. Scientists who believe that birds evolved from dinosaurs hope to find fossils that represent transitional forms—creatures that were part dinosaur and part bird. Many of these have been found, including the feathered dinosaurs of China. Scientists who oppose this idea hope to find fossil evidence linking birds to a different kind of ancient reptile that lived at the same time as the dinosaurs. No such unquestionable ancestor has been found to date.

Step 4. Research by different scientists to *confirm* the hypothesis. Dinosaur and bird paleontologists study the bones of fossil creatures to determine if they are related by evolution. Additional studies of bone structure, teeth, mobility, flight, possible behavior and habits, metabolism, and lifestyle are used to reinforce one argument or the other.

Without undisputed fossil evidence from before the time of *Archaeopteryx*, we must rely on the best specimens available from after its time to shed light on the possible origins of birds. This means looking for birdlike features in dinosaurs and dinosaurlike features in birds, then understanding how one form evolved into the other. Paleontologists have many fossil specimens of dinosaurs and birds after *Archaeopteryx* that show that there were striking similarities between the two. The feathered dinosaurs of China offer especially strong support for an evolutionary link between small meat-eating dinosaurs and birds. This and other evidence mentioned in the preceding pages strongly support the hypothesis that birds evolved from dinosaurs.

Chapter 6

Extinction of the Dinosaurs

Except for the survival of birds, the last of the dinosaurs became extinct 65 million years ago. However, dinosaurs did not disappear because they were evolutionary failures. Dinosaurs were one of the most successful forms of life ever to inhabit our planet. They ruled the earth for 160 million years. By comparison, humans and even our most distant relatives have been around for only about 4 million years.

Extinction is the irreversible elimination of an entire species of plant or animal. Once it occurs, there is no turning back. It is also a natural process. More than 99 percent of all the species of organisms that have ever lived are now extinct.[1]

Although the dinosaurs existed for so many millions of years, most species existed for only a few million years at a time, until they became extinct or evolved into "improved" versions that adapted to changes in the environment. To say that all the dinosaurs became extinct at the end of the

Cretaceous Period is incorrect—most kinds of dinosaurs had already come and gone by then. There is no denying, though, that a mass extinction occurred at the end of the Cretaceous that wiped out about 65 to 70 percent of all animal life.[2] Even those groups of animals that survived—including frogs, lizards, turtles, salamanders, birds, insects, fish, crocodiles, alligators, and mammals—lost great numbers of their species.

Chief among the causes of animal extinction are environmental changes that affect their food supply or body chemistry (such as sustained changes in climate temperature), disease, and natural disasters (such as volcanic eruptions, earthquakes, and the changing surface of the earth). Extensive hunting by natural enemies may also contribute to extinction. Humankind, for example, has hunted many animals such as the buffalo to extinction or near extinction.

Why did the last of the dinosaurs become extinct? This is a great mystery of science.

The death of the dinosaurs is difficult to explain because dinosaurs were part of a strangely selective extinction event. Any suitable explanation must account for the disappearance of dinosaurs as well as flying reptiles, reptiles that swam in the oceans, and ammonites and other sea creatures, including some types of clams, mollusks, and plankton. It must also explain why so many other types of animals continued to thrive after the extinction of the dinosaurs.

Paleontologists disagree on the causes of dinosaur extinction and the length of time it took for this mass dying to occur. There are many theories about what happened. They come in two basic varieties: gradual causes and sudden causes.

Gradual causes would have required millions of years of change. Some possible gradual causes include global climate changes (warming or cooling), volcanic action, shifting continents, overpopulation, poisoning by flowering plants, and the rise of egg-stealing mammals.

Sudden or catastrophic causes would have taken no longer than a few years to wipe out the dinosaurs. One of the most popular extinction theories concerns the collision of an asteroid or comet with Earth.

So far, no single extinction theory can fully explain the great dying at the end of the age of dinosaurs. Evidence has been mounting in favor of the asteroid theory. But a collision with an asteroid may have been only the final blow in a gradual extinction that had been mounting for many years. The asteroid theory also fails to explain why the extinction was so selective. Why did marine reptiles die but most fish survive? Why did dinosaurs of all sizes disappear but birds continue to thrive? There are still many questions to answer before scientists fully understand this great mystery.

Theories of Dinosaur Extinction

THEORY	TYPE OF THEORY	PROBLEMS WITH THE THEORY
The Big Rumble ꜱoke and dust spewed by mass volᴄic eruptions shrouded the earth in ᴋness, killing plants, poisoning ᴇ air and water, and causing the cliᴇte to cool.	Gradual	Does not explain why other land- and ocean-dwelling animals survived.
Shifting Continents ᴀnetary cooling caused by shifting ᴄntinents and changes to the earth's ᴇans.	Gradual	This happened very slowly. Why couldn't dinosaurs and marine reptiles have adapted to the climate change or moved to warmer climates?
Pesky Mammals ᴇw mammals stole and ate ᴅnosaur eggs.	Gradual	Does not explain why some sea life became extinct or why other egg-laying land animals such as snakes and lizards survived. Also, small mammals coexisted with dinosaurs for many millions of year without this happening.
Flower Poisoning ᴏwers first appeared during the ᴄetaceous Period. Were dinosaurs ᴀble to adapt to the chemical ᴀkeup of this new source of food?	Gradual	Plant-eating dinosaurs actually increased in diversity and numbers during the rise of the flowering plants.
Bombardment from Space ᴀpact by an asteroid or comet ᴄrouded the earth in darkness from ᴅbris thrown into the atmosphere ᴅd may have poisoned the air. ᴀnts died and the climate cooled.	Sudden	Although theory is favored today by scientists, it does not explain the survival of some land reptiles, mammals, birds, amphibians, and plants, or why certain ocean life perished but not others.
Supernova ᴘplosion of a nearby star bathed ᴇ earth in deadly cosmic rays.	Sudden	Why did some life-forms die and not others?

CHAPTER 7

MAJOR DISCOVERIES

This chapter summarizes the major discoveries related to the study of the link between dinosaurs and birds. It chronicles the most important specimens that have been discovered, when and where they were found, and the people who first described them scientifically. Notice that the majority of these important discoveries took place after 1990. The study of fossil birds and birdlike dinosaurs is booming in paleontology.

◆ ◆ ◆

1861 (Germany)—One of the smallest dinosaurs ever discovered, *Compsognathus* ("delicate jaw") was only about the size of a chicken. Described by **J. Andreas Wagner**, this small dinosaur was found in the same limestone deposits in which *Archaeopteryx* would be found shortly thereafter. Except for the lack of feather impressions, *Compsognathus* is remarkably similar to *Archaeopteryx*. It was also the first relatively complete specimen of a meat-eating dinosaur ever discovered.

1861 (Germany)—*Archaeopteryx* ("ancient wing"), the first known bird, was named by **Hermann von Meyer**. There are now seven known specimens of *Archaeopteryx*, the most recent of which was discovered in 1992. Found during the early years of dinosaur science, it was one of the first compelling fossils to suggest that birds and dinosaurs are closely related. All specimens of *Archaeopteryx* have been discovered in the fine-grained limestone deposits of the Solnhofen region of Bavaria in Germany. This preservation has sometimes retained the patterns of feathers that once adorned the body. Although considered a bird, *Archaeopteryx* still had reptilian features such as teeth.

1890 (United States)—*Ornithomimus* ("bird mimic") was named by American paleontologist **Othniel Charles Marsh**. Although based on only a fragmented specimen, his description likened the hind leg to that of an ostrich. The discovery of more complete specimens in years to come showed that this dinosaur had other remarkable similarities to the ostrich, including a long neck and toothless beak, a rarity in dinosaurs. *Ornithomimus* is unrelated to modern-day ostriches and the small, feathered dinosaurs that may have given rise to modern birds. It is nonetheless an intriguing example of how evolution can take similar turns millions of years apart to produce this dinosaur and modern flightless birds with similar anatomy.

1922 (Canada)—The first described dromaeosaur, *Dromaeosaurus* ("swift lizard"), was christened by **William D.**

Matthew and **Barnum Brown**. It is one of the kinds of dinosaurs thought to be most closely related to birds.

1922–1924 (Mongolia)—A fossil hunting expedition headed by **Roy Chapman Andrews** of the American Museum of Natural History discovered the first positive evidence of dinosaur nests and eggs, characteristics also associated with birds. In 1923, the explorers discovered the remains of the small theropod dinosaur *Oviraptor* in close proximity to egg nests. At the time is was believed that *Oviraptor*, whose name means "egg thief," was probably gobbling down the eggs of a plant-eating dinosaur. However, in 1994, **Mark Norell** and his colleagues from the American Museum of Natural History revealed that some of the eggs contained the remains of *Oviraptor* embryos, making these the first theropod eggs positively associated with a specific dinosaur.[1]

Another important theropod discovered by the team in 1923 was the small dromaeosaur *Velociraptor* ("swift thief"). One of its sickle claws was found in association with its well-preserved skull, but no one could tell that the claw came from one of its feet. The true nature of this killing machine was unknown until later specimens were found in the 1960s.

Finally, the expedition also uncovered an excellent specimen of *Saurornitholestes* ("lizard bird-robber") which was related to the North American predatory dinosaur *Troodon* named in 1856 (based solely on a tooth). *Velociraptor*, *Oviraptor*, and *Saurornitholestes* were part of the three families of small meat-eating dinosaurs now believed to be most closely related to birds.

✦ ✦ ✦

1969 (United States)—John Ostrom of Yale University described *Deinonychus* ("terrible claw"), a dromaeosaur discovered in Montana. The birdlike features of this dinosaur inspired Ostrom to do a close comparative study of the anatomy of *Archaeopteryx* and *Deinonychus*. Ostrom concluded that birds were the descendants of dinosaurs, and that some birds probably evolved from the family of dromaeosaur dinosaurs. His work was responsible for starting the modern debate about the evolutionary link between dinosaurs and birds.

✦ ✦ ✦

1970 (Central Asia)—Russian paleontologist **Alexander G. Sharov** described a small archosaurian reptile from the Late Triassic Period of Central Asia. Named *Longisquama* ("long scale"), the four-legged creature had a series of long plumelike structures on its back. There was some speculation at the time that these structures were primitive feathers. If that were true, then this animal could have been related to feathered dinosaurs and birds that appeared 90 million years later. However, this idea was dismissed when the structures were thought to be elongated scales, not feathers. This controversy heated up again in 2000, but without any agreement among rival scientific groups. It is still generally accepted that the structures on the back of *Longisquama* are not feathers.

1992 (China)—The Early Cretaceous bird *Sinornis* from China was named by **Paul Sereno** of the University of Chicago and **Chenggang Rao** of the Beijing Museum of Natural History. It dates from 135 million years ago and is one of the earliest known unambiguous birds. It had shed many of the reptilian or dinosaurian features seen in *Archaeopteryx*, making its body plan much closer to that of modern birds.

1993 (Mongolia)—A team from the American Museum of Natural History described the unusual fossil of a flightless bird they named *Mononykus* ("one claw"). This small animal measured only 3 feet (0.9 meter) long and was originally thought to be a theropod dinosaur. Instead of fully developed wings, it had a single claw on each of two short and stout arms. It had slender legs and a long tail and lived 75 million years ago. Originally named *Mononychus*, the spelling had to be changed because the name was already taken by a beetle. It was named by **Altangerel Perle, Mark Norell, Luis Chiappe,** and **James Clark.**

Mononykus was discovered in Mongolia in 1993.

1995 (China)—The Early Cretaceous bird *Confuciusornis* ("Confucius' bird") was first discovered. It has been found in such great numbers since then that it is now the best known bird from this period. Named by **Lianhai Hou, Zhonghe Zhou**, and **Jiang Yong Zhang**, this early bird has a body like *Archaeopteryx* and a skull more like other early birds.

1996 (China)—The Early Cretaceous bird *Liaoningornis* was named by **Lianhai Hou**. This early bird was more advanced in some ways than birds that came after it. It had a keeled breastbone like today's birds. Critics of the dinosaur-bird link cite *Liaoningornis* as an example of a bird that had already taken giant evolutionary steps forward not long after *Archaeopteryx*, suggesting that its roots could be much more ancient than would be expected of a link to dinosaurs.

1996 (Spain)—A fossil bird about the size of a sparrow was named by paleontologists **Jose L. Sanz, Luis Chiappe, B. P. Perez-Moreno, A. D. Buscalioni, J. J. Moratalla, F. Ortega**, and **F. J. Payato-Ariza**. Called *Eoalulavis* ("early little wing bird), it has many important evolutionary advancements in the development of flight, including the first known alula, a group of feathers on the front edge of the bird's wing that helped sustain lift as it flew slowly.

1996 (Mongolia)—A team of paleontologists working in Mongolia discovered the remains of an *Oviraptor* that was brooding over a nest of fifteen to twenty-two eggs. This was the first direct evidence that dinosaurs cared for their young. It also showed that nesting behavior existed in some dinosaurs long before the appearance of modern birds. The discovery was made by scientists from the American Museum of Natural History and the Mongolian Academy of Sciences.

✦ ✦ ✦

1996 (China)—*Sinosauropteryx*, the first dinosaur discovered with a downy coating, was described by **Ji Qiang** and **Ji Shuan**. It was discovered in the Liaoning region of northeastern China. The site has continued to yield many fantastic discoveries of ancient birds and feathered dinosaurs.

✦ ✦ ✦

1997 (Argentina)—Argentine paleontologists **Fernando Novas** and **P. F. Puerta** described the remains of *Unenlagia* ("half bird"), a meat-eating dinosaur that had arms that could fold close to its body like wings. It represents an evolutionary stage in the development of wings between meat-eating dinosaurs and birds.

1998 (China)—Two more spectacular fossils from the Liaoning region of China, *Protarchaeopteryx* and *Caudipteryx*, were described by **Ji Qiang**, **Philip J. Currie**, **Mark Norell**, and **Ji Shuan**. The specimens clearly show the impressions of feathers. These were the first unambiguously feathered dinosaurs ever discovered. These discoveries suggest that feathers evolved prior to the evolution of flight in birds and may have first had another purpose, possibly for keeping the dinosaur warm.

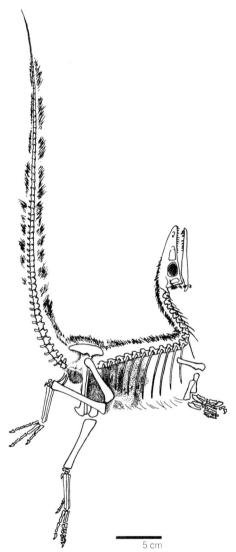

5 cm

Sinosauropteryx prima   MW/SKREPNICK 1997

This is the skeleton of *Sinosauropteryx*, as it was found on the original slab in China.

1998 (Madagascar)—The fossils of a medium-sized bird called *Rahonavis* was described by **Catherine A. Forster, Scott D. Sampson, Luis M. Chiappe, and David W. Krause.** Found in Late Cretaceous deposits in Madagascar, the bird had a sickle claw on the second toe of each foot that is similar to that found on dromaeosaur dinosaurs. It is a good example of a bird with dinosaurlike features.

1999 (China)—Yet another feathered dinosaur emerged from Liaoning, China. In this case, it was a member of the rare theropod family called therizinosaurs. Paleontologists **Xu Xing, Tang Zhilu, and Wang Xiaolin** called it *Beipiaosaurus.* It had a downy coating on its arms, legs, and shoulders much like *Sinosauropteryx.*

1999 (China)—*Sinornithosaurus,* a dromaeosaur with protofeathers, was found in Early Cretaceous deposits of China and described by **Xu Xing, Wang Xiaolin, and Wu Xiaochun.** It was the first member of this family of dinosaurs to show evidence of a downy coating on its body. It is the oldest specimen of a dromaeosaur yet described. Its shoulder shows adaptations that would later be used by birds for powered flight. It is evidence that flight in birds evolved from the ground up.

2000 (United States)—*Bambiraptor,* a dromaeosaur, was found in Montana and described by **David A. Burnham,**

Nomingia was discovered in the Gobi Desert.

Kraig L. Derstler, Philip J. Currie, Robert T. Bakker, Zhonghe Zhou, and John H. Ostrom. It includes several birdlike features, including a wishbone and shoulder bones that appear to be stepping-stones to the design of wings in birds. This dinosaur lived during the Late Cretaceous Period.

2000 (Mongolia)—*Nomingia* ("from the Nomingiin," a part of the Gobi Desert), an oviraptorid dinosaur, was discovered with a pygostyle—the kind of tailbone found in birds. Prior to this, a pygostyle had never been seen in a dinosaur. *Nomingia* was described by **Rinchen Barsbold, Halszka Osmólska, Mahito Watabe, Philip J. Currie,** and **Khishigjaw Tsogtbaatar.**

2000 (China)—*Microraptor*, the smallest feathered dinosaur yet discovered, was found in Liaoning Province. Named by Chinese paleontologists **Xu Xing, Zhonghe Zhou,** and **Wang Xiaolin**, *Microraptor* is only about the size of a crow, making it smaller than *Archaeopteryx*, the first bird. The specimen has evidence of feathers on its lower limbs but does not have wings. The discovery is important because it has been generally assumed that birds evolved from small meat-eating dinosaurs, yet evidence for such small dinosaurs has been slim. *Microraptor* shows that small dinosaurs with many similarities to birds did exist.

CHAPTER NOTES

Chapter 1. Dinosaurs and Birds

1. Stephen Jay Gould, ed., *The Book of Life* (New York: W. W. Norton & Company, 1993), pp. 67–68.

2. David E. Fastovsky and David B. Weishampel, *The Evolution and Extinction of the Dinosaurs* (Cambridge, England: Cambridge University Press, 1996), pp. 294–298.

3. James O. Farlow and Michael K. Brett-Surman, eds., *The Complete Dinosaur* (Bloomington, Ind.: Indiana University Press, 1997), p. 230.

4. Philip J. Currie and Kevin Padian, eds., *The Encyclopedia of Dinosaurs* (San Diego, Calif.: Academic Press, 1997), pp. 32–33.

Chapter 2. The Kinds of Dinosaurs and Where They Lived

1. David B. Weishampel, Peter Dodson, and Halszka Osmólska, eds., *The Dinosauria* (Berkeley, Calif.: University of California Press, 1990), p. 11.

2. Paul Sereno, "The Evolution of Dinosaurs," *Science*, June 25, 1999, vol. 284, p. 2137.

3. Ibid.

4. David E. Fastovsky and David B. Weishampel, *The Evolution and Extinction of the Dinosaurs* (Cambridge, England: Cambridge University Press, 1996), pp. 272–273.

5. Xu Xing, Zhonghe Zhou, and Wang Xiaolin, "The Smallest Known Non-Avian Theropod Dinosaur," *Nature*, no. 408, December 7, 2000, pp. 705–708.

6. James O. Farlow and Michael K. Brett-Surman, eds., *The Complete Dinosaur* (Bloomington, Ind.: Indiana University Press, 1997), pp. 242, 271–272.

7. Peter Dodson, *The Horned Dinosaurs* (Princeton: Princeton University Press, 1996), p. 10.

Chapter 3. The Origin and Evolution of Birds

1. David E. Fastovsky and David B. Weishampel, *The Evolution and Extinction of the Dinosaurs* (Cambridge, England: Cambridge University Press, 1996), p. 314.

2. Gregory S. Paul, ed., *The Scientific American Book of Dinosaurs* (New York: St. Martin's Press, 2000), p. 200.

3. Fastovsky and Weishampel, p. 313.

4. Ji Qiang, Philip J. Currie, Mark A. Norell, and Ji Shuan, "Two Feathered Dinosaurs from Northeastern China," *Nature*, no. 393, June 25, 1998, p. 761.

Chapter 4. Feathered Dinosaurs

1. Thom Holmes, "Dinosaur or Bird? The 'Feathered' Wonder." *Dino Times*, vol. 7, no. 3, March 1997, pp. 1, 3.

2. Thom Holmes, "A Dinosaur with Feathers?" *Dino Times*, vol. 6, no. 12, December 1996, pp. 1, 3.

3. Thom Holmes, "Update on the Feathered Dinosaur from China." *Dino Times*, vol. 7, no. 6, June 1997, p. 3.

4. Terry D. Jones, James O. Farlow, John A. Ruben, Donald M. Henderson, and Willem J. Hillenius, "Cursoriality in Bipedal Archosaurs," *Nature*, no. 406, August 17, 2000, pp. 716–718.

5. Ji Qiang, Philip J. Currie, Mark A. Norell, and Ji Shuan, "Two Feathered Dinosaurs from Northeastern China," *Nature*, no. 393, June 25, 1998, p. 761.

6. Xu Xing, Tang Zhilu, Wang Xiaolin, "A Therizinosaur Dinosaur with Integumentary Structures from China," *Nature*, no. 399, May 27, 1999, pp. 350–354.

7. Xu Xing, Wang Xiaolin, and Wu Xiaochun, "A Dromaeosaurid Dinosaur with a Filamentous Integument from the Yixian Formation of China," *Nature*, no. 401, pp. 262–266.

8. Ji Qiang, Mark A. Norell, Gao Ke-Qin, Ji Shuan, and Ren Dong, "The Distribution of Integumentary Structures in a Feathered Dinosaur," *Nature*, no. 410, April 25, 2001, pp. 1084–1088.

Chapter 5. Are Birds Descended from Dinosaurs?

1. Xu Xing, Zhonghe Zhou, Wang Xiaolin, "The Smallest Known Non-Avian Theropod Dinosaur," *Nature*, no. 408, December 7, 2000, pp. 705–708.

2. Rinchen Barsbold, Halszka Osmólska, Mahito Watabe, Philip J. Currie, and Khishigjaw Tsogtbaatar, "New Oviraptorosaur (Dinosauria, Theropoda) from Mongolia: The First Dinosaur with a Pygostyle," *Acta Palaeontologica Polonica*, 2000, no. 45 (2), pp. 97–106.

3. Mark A. Norell, Peter Makovicky, and James M. Clark, "A Velociraptor Wishbone," *Nature*, no. 389, October 2, 1997, p. 447.

4. Fernando E. Novas and P. F. Puerta, "New Evidence Concerning Avian Origins from the Late Cretaceous of Patagonia," *Nature*, no. 387, pp. 390–392.

5. Catherine A. Forster, Scott D. Sampson, Luis M. Chiappe, and David W. Krause, "The Theropod Ancestry of Birds: New Evidence form the Late Cretaceous of Madagascar," *Science*, vol. 279, March 20, 1998, pp. 1915–1919.

6. James O. Farlow and Michael K. Brett-Surman, eds., *The Complete Dinosaur* (Bloomington, Ind.: Indiana University Press, 1997), p. 230.

7. David E. Fastovsky and David B. Weishampel, *The Evolution and Extinction of the Dinosaurs* (Cambridge, England: Cambridge University Press, 1996), p. 297.

8. David A. Burnham, Kraig L. Derstler, Philip J. Currie, Robert T. Bakker, Zhonghe Zhou, and John H. Ostrom, "Remarkable New Birdlike Dinosaur (Theropoda: Maniraptora) From the Upper Cretaceous of Montana," *The University of Kansas Paleontological Contributions*, no. 13, March 15, 2000, pp. 1–14.

9. Barsbold, Osmólska, Watabe, Currie, and Tsogtbaatar, pp. 97–106.

10. Novas and Puerta, pp. 390–392.

11. Burnham, Derstler, Currie, Bakker, Zhou, and Ostrom, pp. 1–14.

12. Hans C. E. Larsson, Paul C. Sereno, and Jeffrey A. Wilson, "Forebrain Enlargement among Nonavian Theropod Dinosaurs," *Journal of Vertebrate Paleontology*, vol. 20, no. 3, September, 2000, pp. 615–618.

13. Terry D. Jones, John A. Ruben, Larry D. Martin, Evgeny N. Kurochkin, Alan Feduccia, Paul F. A. Maderson, Willem J. Hillenius, Nichols R. Geist, and Vladimir Alifanov, "Nonavian Feathers in a Late Triassic Archosaur," *Science*, vol. 288, June 23, 2000, pp. 2202–2205.

14. Robert R. Reisz, Hans-Dieter Sues, "The 'Feathers' of *Longisquama*," *Nature*, vol. 408 (6811), p. 428.

15. Sankar Chatterjee, "Cranial Anatomy and Relationships of a New Triassic Bird from Texas," *Philosophical Transactions of the Royal Society (Biological Sciences)*, 332 (1265), pp. 277–346.

16. Fastovsky and Weishampel, p. 298.

Chapter 6. Extinction of the Dinosaurs

1. David M. Raup, *Extinction: Bad Genes or Bad Luck?* (New York: W. W. Norton, 1991), pp. 3–4.

2. Ibid., p. 71.

Chapter 7. Major Discoveries

1. Mark A. Norell, J. M. Clark, D. Demberelyin, B. Rinchen, Luis M. Chiappe, A. R. Davidson, M. C. McKenna, P. Altangerel, and Michael J. Novacek, "A Theropod Dinosaur Embryo and the Affinities of the Flaming Cliffs Dinosaur Eggs," *Science*, vol. 266, pp. 779–782.

GLOSSARY

archosaur—A subclass of Reptilia including crocodilians, dinosaurs (with birds), pterosaurs, and thecodonts.

bilateral symmetry—A feature of vertebrate body design in which one side of the body is a mirror image of the other.

bipedal—Walking on two legs.

carnivore—A meat-eating creature.

Ceratopsia—"Horned face." The order of horned dinosaurs that includes the psittacosaurs, protoceratopsids, and ceratopsids.

ceratopsids—The family of ceratopsians that includes the horned dinosaurs such as *Triceratops*.

chordate—An animal with a backbone, including that with the precursor of the backbone called the notochord.

classification—A traditional system of classifying organisms based on their similarities in form. The hierarchy of this classification method is kingdom, phylum, class, order, family, genus, species.

convergent evolution—The independent evolution of similar anatomical features by different kinds of animals. The evolution of wings and powered flight in bats, pterosaurs, and birds is an example.

Cretaceous Period—The third and final major time division (144 to 65 million years ago) of the Mesozoic Era. The end of the age of dinosaurs.

digit—A finger or toe.

dromaeosaur—"Running lizard." Small- to medium-sized meat-eating dinosaurs. Dromaeosaurs had claws on their second toes that they used to slash at prey.

evolution—The patterns of change through time of living organisms.

extinction—The irreversible elimination of an entire species of plant or animal.

furcula—The wishbone found in birds. It helped the wings connect to the shoulder and breast bones. Furculae have also been found in the skeletons of some dinosaurs.

herbivore—A plant-eating creature.

Jurassic Period—The second of the three major time divisions (208 to 144 million years ago) of the Mesozoic Era.

Mesozoic Era—The age of reptiles spanning from 245 to 65 million years ago. Dinosaurs lived during the era from about 225 to 65 million years ago.

Ornithischia—One of two orders of dinosaurs grouped by hip structure. Ornithischians had a hip with a backward-pointing pubis bone.

ornithopods—A group of two-footed ornithischian, plant-eating dinosaurs.

oviraptor—"Egg thief." Small birdlike theropod with strong arms, long hand claws, a toothless beak, and two small pointed teeth in the roof of its mouth.

paleontologist—A scientist who studies life-forms of the geologic past, especially through the analysis of plant and animal fossils.

powered flight—The ability of a creature to fly under its own power by flapping its wings, as in birds, bats, and pterosaurs.

predator—A creature that kills other creatures for food.

protoceratopsids—"First horned face." A family of the Ceratopsians that includes small frilled dinosaurs lacking nose and brow horns, such as *Protoceratops*.

protofeathers—Possible early evolutionary stage of feathers consisting of fiberlike filaments seen in some fossil dinosaurs.

psittacosaurs—"Parrot lizards." A family of the Ceratopsians representing the earliest members of this group, such as *Psittacosaurus*.

pterosaur—A flying reptile that lived during the Mesozoic Era.

pygostyle—The pointed, stubby tailbone of birds. Pygostyles have also been found in the skeletons of some dinosaurs.

Saurischia—One of two orders of dinosaurs grouped by hip structure. Saurischians had a hip with a forward-pointing pubis bone.

sauropod—Large plant-eating saurischian dinosaurs with long necks and long tails.

sexual dimorphism—Differences in size and shape between males and females of the same kind of animal.

synsacrum—In birds, a single bony structure that joins the hip to the back bones.

therizinosaur—Mysterious, poorly known group of meat-eating dinosaurs with long hand claws, robust limbs, and often large bodies. At least one specimen appears to have had feathers (*Beipiaosaurus*).

theropod—Any of a group of saurischian dinosaurs that ate meat and walked on two legs.

Triassic Period—The first of the three major time divisions (245 to 208 million years ago) of the Mesozoic Era.

vertebra—A bone of the neck, spine, or tail.

vertebrate—Any animal that has a backbone (spine).

wishbone—See *furcula*.

FURTHER READING

Even though there have been hundreds of books about dinosaurs published, reputable dinosaur books are hard to find. Listed here are some of the authors' favorites. They range from the examination of individual kinds of dinosaurs to several encyclopedic volumes covering a wide range of dinosaur-related topics. A number of history books are included in the list as well to help those who are interested in the lives and times of paleontologists.

Bakker, Robert T. *The Dinosaur Heresies.* New York: William Morrow and Company, 1986.

Bishop, Nic. *Digging for Bird-Dinosaurs: An Expedition to Madagascar.* New York: Houghton Mifflin Co., 2000.

Carpenter, Kenneth. *Eggs, Nests, and Baby Dinosaurs.* Bloomington, Ind.: University Press, 1999.

Chatterjee, Sankar. *The Rise of Birds.* Baltimore, Md.: Johns Hopkins University Press, 1997.

Colbert, Edwin H. *The Great Dinosaur Hunters and Their Discoveries.* New York: Dover Publications, 1984.

Dixon, Dougal, Barry Cox, R. J. G. Savage, and Brian Gardiner. *The Macmillan Illustrated Encyclopedia of Dinosaurs and Other Prehistoric Animals.* New York: Macmillan, 1988.

Farlow, James O., and Michael K. Brett-Surman (eds.). *The Complete Dinosaur.* Bloomington, Ind.: University Press, 1997.

Feduccia, Alan. *The Origin and Evolution of Birds*. New Haven, Conn.: Yale University Press, 1996.

Gallagher, William B. *When Dinosaurs Roamed New Jersey*. New Brunswick, N.J.: Rutgers University Press, 1997.

Holmes, Thom. *Fossil Feud: The Rivalry of the First American Dinosaur Hunters*. Parsippany, N.J.: Julian Messner, 1998.

Horner, John R., and James Gorman. *Digging Dinosaurs*. New York: Workman Publishing Co., Inc., 1988.

Norell, Mark A., Eugene S. Gaffney, and Lowell Dingus. *Discovering Dinosaurs*. New York: Alfred A. Knopf, 1995.

Norman, David. *The Illustrated Encyclopedia of Dinosaurs*. London: Salamander Books, 1985.

Russell, Dale A. *The Dinosaurs of North America: An Odyssey in Time*. Minocqua, Wis.: NorthWord Press, 1989.

Shipman, Pat. *Taking Wing: Archaeopteryx and the Evolution of Bird Flight*. New York: Simon & Schuster, 1998.

Sloan, Christopher. *Feathered Dinosaurs*. Washington, D.C.: National Geographic Society, 2000.

Spalding, David A. *Dinosaur Hunters*. Rocklin, Calif.: Prima Publishing, 1993.

Sternberg, Charles H. *Life of a Fossil Hunter*. New York: Dover, 1990.

Weishampel, David B., and Luther Young. *Dinosaurs of the East Coast*. Baltimore, Md.: Johns Hopkins University Press, 1996.

INTERNET ADDRESSES

American Museum of Natural History. *Fossil Halls.* <http://www.amnh.org/exhibitions/Fossil_Halls>.

Jacobson, Russ. *Dino Russ's Lair: Dinosaur and Vertebrate Paleontology Information.* <http://www.isgs.uiuc.edu/dinos/dinos_home.html>.

National Geographic Society. *Dinosaur Eggs.* <http://www.nationalgeographic.com/dinoeggs>.

The Natural History Museum, London. *Dinosaur Data Files.* <http://www.nhm.ac.uk/education/online/dinosaur_data_files.html>.

Scotese, Christopher R. *Paleomap Project.* <http://www.scotese.com>.

Smithsonian Institution. *Paleobiology.* <http://www.nmnh.si.edu/paleo/index.html> (February 26, 2001).

Summer, Edward. *The Dinosaur Interplanetary Gazette.* <http://www.dinosaur.org/frontpage.html>.

Tyrrell Museum of Palaeontology, Alberta. *Dinosaur Hall.* <http://www.tyrrellmuseum.com/tour/dinohall.html>.

University of Bristol. *Dinobase.* <http://palaeo.gly.bris.ac.uk/dinobase/dinopage.html>.

University of California, Berkeley, Museum of Paleontology. *The Dinosauria: Truth Is Stranger Than Fiction.* <http://www.ucmp.berkeley.edu/diapsids/dinosaur.html>.

INDEX

111